Club Law Manual

by

Kenneth W Pain, B.Sc., Barrister

London
Callow Publishing
2005

ISBN 1 898899 78 9

Every care is taken in the preparation of this publication, but the author and publishers cannot accept responsibility for the consequences of any error, however caused.

Printed and Bound in Great Britain by MPG Books Ltd, Bodmin, Cornwall.

Published by Callow Publishing Limited,
4 Shillingford Street,
London N1 2DP
www.callowpublishing.com

Club Law Manual

CALLOW PUBLISHING

Preface

Over the years many people have pointed out that it is difficult to find a simple guide to the law as it affects members' clubs. There are, of course, several works that contain information relevant to members' clubs and the way they operate, but for club managers and their advisers to find the relevant parts is not always easy. This has encouraged me to write this manual on club law. The advent of the Licensing Act 2003 has presented me with the ideal opportunity.

The book concentrates on member' clubs and the numerous laws that affect how they are managed, the statutory authorities that have an interest in them, and the relationships between officers, members and the clubs themselves. The guidance is not limited to the provisions of the Licensing Act 2003. Other important legislation, dealing with employment, food hygiene, health and safety and public liability are also covered. General advice in relation to the proper conduct of meetings and formulating club rules is also offered.

The opening chapters of the book focus on the Licensing Act 2003 and the controls it introduces in relation to the supply of alcohol and the provision of many types of entertainment. There are few references to case law because much of the existing case law will no longer be relevant once the new Act is in full force. Many of the provisions of the Licensing Act 2003 will, I have no doubt, be interpreted by the High Court in due course but, for the time being, the words of the statute are the best guide we have.

I hope this book will be useful to practitioners, to all those concerned in running clubs, to the police and the statutory authorities, and not least to the new licensing committees of the local authorities. I hope it is sufficiently readable to be of assistance to those who have taken on the running and management of members' clubs.

The book does not answer every question that may arise in relation to members' clubs. Complex or unusual problems are beyond the scope of the book, but I am confident that most aspects of club management are touched upon, and that where the text does not give a comprehensive answer, enough information is given to enable the reader to find other, more detailed, advice fairly easily. My aim has been to present the information in a way that will enable busy people to find what they are looking for quickly.

Inevitably, in a work that features entirely new law, some of the views expressed are my own. As case law develops, some of those views may prove to be incorrect, but I believe they are soundly based on experience.

Since the provisions of the Licensing Act 2003 on transitional applications came into effect on 7 February 2005, Chapters 1 and 3 are of most importance to readers coming to grips with the new licensing regime. I recommend that these two chapters be studied with some urgency. Other aspects of the new law can then be examined at a more leisurely pace.

Although the text of the book is based on the Act of 2003, it is important to remember that until the second appointed day (still to be designated as this book goes to press), when the Act will come into full force, new applications for club registration certificates are still to be made to the magistrates following the procedures in section 41 of, and Schedule 5 to, the Licensing Act 1964. Since those procedures will become obsolete soon, they are not covered in this work.

KWP
March 2005

Contents

Contents

Table of References

Chapter 1

Introduction

1.   The Members' Club

The first question to be addressed is what, exactly, is a members' club, and how does it differ from other clubs? The answer is that, unlike a nightclub or other commercially run club, such as a sports or leisure club, a members' club does not have a proprietor who derives a livelihood from the activities carried on in the club. A members' club consists of an association of like-minded people who come together to establish premises that can be used by them to further the interests they share. Golf clubs, tennis clubs, works staff clubs and political clubs are examples of members' clubs.

Often, a members' club is described as a club that is run by its members for the benefit of its members in general. Apart from those who may be employed by the club, no individual derives financial benefit from the activities of the club. All assets belong to the members generally, and all profits accrue for the benefit of the members or for any charity that the club may choose to support. It is these features, relating to the management of a club, that distinguish a members' club from a proprietary club such as a night club, sports club, or leisure club. If a members' club is dissolved, its assets should be distributed among those who are members at the moment of dissolution, in equal shares, unless the constitution demands that they be passed on to a particular charity or to some other organisation with similar objectives.

2.   Licensable Activities

The next matter to be considered is whether a members' club needs any sort of statutory authority to operate as a club. The answer depends on the activity or activities that the members wish to carry on at their premises. The Licensing Act 2003 refers to "licensable activities". Where the activities to be carried on by a club include licensable activities, then a "club premises certificate", authorising the activities in question, must be obtained from the local licensing authority.

If the members of the club in question do not intend to carry out any activities that are licensable activities, there is no need for a club premises certificate to be obtained. The definition of "licensable activities" includes "the supply of alcohol by or on behalf of a club to, or to the order of, a member of the club", and, since most members' clubs wish to be able, at the very least, to supply intoxicating liquor to members and guests, most need a club premises certificate.

3. The Licensing Act 2003

The Licensing Act 2003 heralds the root-and-branch revision of the law relating to the sale and supply of alcohol and other leisure facilities that successive governments have been promising for the last decade and more. These innovations apply to members' clubs as well as to others in the licensed trade and entertainment industry. Some of the changes introduced were controversial when the Bill was being debated in Parliament, and some of them still give rise to genuine concerns.

It is arguable that the most hotly debated provisions of the Act are those that have the effect of transferring the jurisdiction for the control of liquor licensing from licensing committees comprised of magistrates, to licensing committees made up of councillors who are members of local authorities. Many find it hard to see the benefit of this change, which abandons the wealth of experience of the local magistrates, who are trained in making judicial decisions based on evidence, in favour of new bodies comprised of people who are not, generally, expected to act judicially. Those who will now make up the licensing committees charged with dealing with licensing applications have, quite properly, so far exercised their decision-making powers on the basis of their beliefs in what the local electorate would wish them to do, rather than on the basis of evidence placed before them.

The new role that these councillors are being asked to play

clearly demands that they act judicially. The statute contains provisions for appeals, which make clear that local authority licensing committees are to be the first tier of a judicial structure that, on matters of fact, extends to the Crown Court, via the magistrates' court; and on matters of law, extends to the House of Lords, via the High Court. Local licensing committees will be making judicial decisions and, consequently, the case law relating to the proper exercise of judicial discretion (see page 5) continues to apply.

The requirement to act judicially is of great importance, since any failure to so act will afford an aggrieved applicant a ground to challenge a decision by way of appeal.

4. The Licensing Authority

Section 3 of the Licensing Act provides that the local authorities now having jurisdiction over licensing matters usually are:
- in England, the district council where there is one, or the county council where there is no district council;
- in Wales, the county or county borough;
- in London, the London borough council or the Common Council of the City of London.

An application for a club premises certificate must be submitted to the council having jurisdiction over the area in which the club's premises are situated. Occasionally, premises may be situated in more than one council's area, as where a local authority boundary runs through the buildings that are to be used for licensable activities. Section 12 of the Licensing Act provides that in such a case, the "relevant authority" is the one in whose area the greater or greatest part of the premises is situated. If the greater or greatest part is not in the area of either authority, the applicant must nominate one of them as the relevant authority.

5. The Licensing Objectives

The whole of the Act of 2003 is focused on "licensing objectives". They are the objectives that Parliament had in mind when it passed the legislation. There are four objectives, set out in section 4:
- the prevention of crime and disorder;
- public safety;
- the prevention of public nuisance; and

• the protection of children from harm.

These objectives must be central to the licensing policy that each licensing authority adopts, and a licensing authority's decision in relation to an application must be based on these objectives. Consequently, an authority must, as a general rule, grant an application submitted to it if the application is in the proper form and the applicant is eligible for the certificate or other authorisation applied for. An application may be rejected only if it has not been made properly, or if rejection is necessary in order to promote one or more of the licensing objectives. A licensing authority may impose conditions upon a certificate which it grants but, again, only if the conditions are considered necessary to promote one or more of the licensing objectives, or are consistent with the "club operating schedule" submitted with the application (see Chapter 4).

"Authorised persons", "interested parties" and "responsible authorities" may make representations to the licensing authority in respect of any application submitted (with the exception of an application for conversion made under the transitional provisions contained in the Act; see Chapter 3). If a licensing authority receives a relevant representation, it must, generally, hold a hearing to consider the representation. The applicant may attend the hearing, with a barrister, solicitor or any other person if desired, to respond to the representation. Allowing a person other than a qualified lawyer to speak for a party is a novel provision introduced in regulations made under the Licensing Act 2003; care must be taken to ensure that an unqualified person is competent to deal with the application. Persons who behave in a disruptive manner at a hearing may be asked to leave. The procedures are dealt with in more detail elsewhere in this book, but following such a hearing, the authority must take such steps (if any) as it considers necessary for the promotion of the licensing objectives. It the authority decides that it is not necessary to take any steps for that purpose, it must grant the application.

A licensing authority must focus on the licensing objectives when reaching its decisions. It may not reject an application or impose conditions on a certificate because of some preference of the authority, because it believes that such action would meet the wishes of the electorate, or because of some other whim or fancy. For example, an authority may not fix an arbitrary quota of certificates for an area. The authority must reach its decisions on the basis of the evidence put before it and in accordance with the legislation. Existing case law in relation to the obligation to act judicially remains relevant; see *R v Boteler* – decisions must amount to an exercise of a judicial discretion and not a mere capricious act, regardless of the circumstances of each application; *Sharpe v Wakefield* – decisions must not be arbitrary, vague or fanciful, but legal and regular; and *R v Licensing Justices at North Tyneside, ex parte Todd and Lewis* – each case must be considered on its merits. No rules that fetter the authority's discretion may be laid down.

6. Licensing Policy Statements

When licensing applications are being dealt with, consistency and transparency are matters of primary importance. Under the regime in force before the Licensing Act of 2003, the Magistrates' Association and the Justices' Clerks' Society agreed a guideline document that served to inform individual licensing committees of matters that ought to form the basis of licensing policy statements throughout England and Wales. The Licensing Act 2003, together with the Guidance Document issued in July 2004 by the Secretary of State for Culture Media and Sport, pursuant to section 182 of the Act (see www.culture.gov.uk), both reflect an intention to ensure the continuation of the same degree of consistency and transparency following the transfer of the jurisdiction to the local authorities.

Section 5 of the Act provides that in each period of three years, each licensing authority must:

- determine its policy with respect to the exercise of its licensing functions; and
- publish a statement of that policy by 7 February 2005.

Before determining its policy, each authority must consult, among others:

- the chief officer of police for its area;
- the fire authority for that area;
- persons whom the licensing authority considers to be representative of holders of club premises certificates, and other licences under the 2003 Act, issued by the authority; and
- such other persons as the licensing authority considers to be representative of businesses and residents in its area.

During each three-year period, the licensing authority is required to keep its policy under review, and make such revisions to it, at such times, as it considers appropriate. The obligation to consult applies to revisions of an authority's policy as it does to its original determination of policy. Any revisions must be published, together with a statement of the reasons for them.

One of the concerns about the new procedures is that they allow scope for wide variations between the policy documents published by different authorities. Nevertheless, an individual applicant is most interested in the policy statement for the area in which the relevant premises are situated. A copy can be obtained from the chief executive of the local authority. The contents of the statement may help an applicant avoid issues that could result in the rejection of the application.

The Guidance Document sets out "fundamental principles" that a licensing authority ought to keep in mind when formulating its licensing policy. Those principles include the following:

"3.8 All statements of policy should . . . begin by stating the four licensing objectives, which the licensing policy will be determined with a view to promoting [*sic*]. In determining its policy, a licensing authority must have regard to this Guidance and give appropriate weight to the views of those it has consulted. Having regard to this Guidance will be important for consistency, particularly where licensing authority boundaries meet.

3.9 While statements of policy may set out a general approach to the making of licensing decisions, they must not ignore or be inconsistent with provisions in the 2003 Act. For example, a statement of policy must not undermine the right of an individual to apply under the terms of the 2003 Act for a variety of permissions and to have any such application considered on its individual merits.

3.10 Similarly, no statement of policy should override the right of any person to make representations on an application or to seek a review of a licence or certificate where provision has been made for them to do so in the 2003 Act.

3.11 Statements of policies should make clear that licensing is about regulating the carrying on of licensable activities on licensed premises, by qualifying clubs and at temporary events within the terms of the 2003 Act, and that the conditions attached to various authorisations will be focused on matters which are within the control of individual licensees and others in possession of relevant authorisations. Accordingly, these matters will centre on the premises being used for licensable activities and the vicinity of those premises. . . A statement of policy should also make clear that licensing law is not the primary mechanism for the general control of nuisance and anti-social behaviour by individuals once they are away from the licensed premises and, therefore, beyond the direct control of the individual, club or business holding the licence, certificate or authorisation concerned."

The Guidance Document does not, itself, have the force of law, but licensing authorities are required to have regard to it. Thus, although an authority is not bound to give effect to any recommendation included in the Guidance Document, if it chooses not to, it will have to give full reasons for its actions.

No doubt, at least in the early days of the new legislation, there will be many challenges, by way of applications for judicial review, to local authority decisions concerning the extent to which the authorities are prepared to be constrained by the Guidance.

Chapter 2

Qualifying Clubs

1. General Principles

Under the legislation in force before the Licensing Act 2003, registered members' clubs were dealt with differently from licensed premises. These clubs supplied intoxicating liquor to members and guests on the authority of a registration certificate granted not by the licensing justices, but by magistrates sitting as a magistrates' court. The Act of 2003 contains controls in relation to members' clubs that are much closer to those that apply to other licensed premises. Members' clubs now have to go to the same licensing authority to obtain a certificate for the club's premises and submit an operating schedule, in much the same way as an applicant for a premises licence under the Act. The Act does, though, preserve many of the special provisions that distinguished a registered club from licensed premises in the earlier legislation, but the procedural matters that relate to clubs are now very similar to those that apply to licensed premises.

Some clubs which have in the past operated as members' clubs may now be better off with a premises licence under the new legislation. On the other hand, many such clubs may wish to maintain the character of a members' club, restricting participation in qualifying activities to members and guests, and keeping the management of the club under the control of the members.

2. The Club Premises Certificate

Under the 2003 Act, to be able to supply alcohol, a club must have a "club premises certificate". This means a certificate granted under Part 4 of the Act for premises "occupied by and habitually used for the purposes of a club". A certificate is valid only if granted by the relevant licensing authority. It certifies that:

- the premises may be used by the club for one or more specified "qualifying club activities"; and
- the club is a qualifying club in relation to the activities.

(Licensing Act 2003, section 60.)

"Qualifying club activities" are defined in section 1:

- the supply of alcohol by or on behalf of a club to, or to the order of, a member of the club;
- the sale by retail of alcohol by or on behalf of a club to a guest of a member for consumption on the premises where the sale takes place, and
- the provision of regulated entertainment by or on behalf of a club for members of the club or members and their guests.

The Act goes on specifically to provide that the "supply" of alcohol does not include selling it by retail. A members' club "supplies" rather than sells alcohol to members because, technically, the stock of drinks is already owned, collectively, by the members. A sale occurs only where alcohol that does not belong to the purchaser is given to him in exchange for purchase money.

3.   Conditions of Qualification

Section 61 of the Act sets out the basis on which a club may be considered a "qualifying" club. It provides that a club is a qualifying club in relation to the supply of alcohol to members or guests if it satisfies certain general conditions (set out in section 62) and the additional conditions mentioned in section 64. The general conditions are that:

- under club rules persons may not be admitted to membership or, as candidates for membership, to any of the privileges of membership, without an interval of at least two days between their nomination or application for membership and their admission;
- the rules must provide that persons becoming members without prior nomination or application may not be admitted to the privileges of membership without an interval of at least two days between their becoming members and their admission;
- the club is established and conducted in good faith as a club

(see below);
- the club has at least twenty-five members; and
- alcohol is not supplied, or intended to be supplied, to members on the premises otherwise than by or on behalf of the club.

These conditions are designed to ensure that the club's character is maintained, and that it does not become a public house.

The additional conditions are that:
- the purchase and supply of alcohol, so far as not managed by the club in general meeting or otherwise by the general body of members, must be managed by a committee. This committee must consist of members of the club, aged at least eighteen years, and elected to the committee by the members of the club. (This condition does not apply to industrial and provident societies, friendly societies etc; see below);
- no arrangements are made, or intended to be made, for any person to receive at the expense of the club any commission, percentage or similar payment on or with reference to purchases of alcohol by the club; and
- no arrangements are made, or intended to be made, for any person (directly or indirectly) to derive any pecuniary benefit from the supply of alcohol by or on behalf of the club to members or guests, apart from a benefit to the members collectively from profits that accrue to club funds.

These conditions ensure that the supply of alcohol remains under the control of the members and does not pass into the hands of a single person or group of persons. If it did, the club would, in truth, have a proprietor and the club premises certificate would no longer be appropriate. See also Chapter 8, on club rules.

When a club applies for a club premises certificate, it is required to complete a form of declaration that it meets the qualifying conditions; see page 24.

4. Establishment and Conduct

"Good faith" simply means a *genuine* commitment to the principles that qualify the club for its premises certificate. In determining whether a club is established and conducted in good faith as a club, the licensing authority should take the following matters into account:
- any arrangements restricting the club's freedom of purchase of

alcohol;
- any rule or other arrangement, under which any money or property of the club, or any gain arising from carrying on the club, may be applied otherwise than for the benefit of the club as a whole, or for charitable, benevolent or political purposes;
- the arrangements for giving members information about the finances of the club;
- the books of account and other records kept to ensure the accuracy of the financial information given to members; and
- the nature of the premises to be occupied by the club.

If a licensing authority decides that a club does not satisfy the requirement of being established and conducted in good faith, it must give the club notice of that decision and the reasons for it. (Licensing Act 2003, section 63.)

5. Registered Societies

Certain types of association have, for historical reasons, been given a special status. Generally, they are organisations which, because they provide for certain categories of employee, or for socio-economic reasons, have been considered to warrant special status in law. Such groups include industrial and provident societies, friendly societies, and miners' welfare institutes.

Section 65 of the Licensing Act concerns industrial and provident societies and friendly societies. Societies registered under the Industrial and Provident Societies Act 1965, the Friendly Societies Act 1974 and the Friendly Societies Act 1992 are taken to satisfy the first additional condition listed above (concerning the purchase and supply of alcohol), if, and to the extent that, the purchase of alcohol for the club and the supply of alcohol by the club are under the control of the members or a committee appointed by the members.

Generally, the Licensing Act applies to incorporated friendly societies in the same way as it applies to clubs. Consequently, society premises are treated as club premises, society members are treated as if they were club members, and anything done by or on behalf of the society is to be treated as if it were done by or on behalf of a club.

Section 65 provides that, when deciding whether an incorporated friendly society is a qualifying club in relation to a qualifying club activity, the society is to be taken to satisfy:

- the general condition concerning establishment and conduct in good faith;
- the general condition that alcohol is not supplied, or intended to be supplied, to members on the premises other than by or on behalf of the club; and
- the three additional conditions set out on page 10.

6. Miners' Welfare Institutes

Section 66 of the Licensing Act 2003 concerns miners' welfare institutes. As a general rule, "relevant miners' welfare institutes" are treated as clubs for the purposes of the Act. In particular, institute premises are treated as club premises, enrolled members are considered to be club members, and anything done by or on behalf of the trustees or managers is treated as if it had been done by or on behalf of a club.

In determining whether an institute is a qualifying club in relation to a qualifying club activity, the institute is to be taken to satisfy:
- the general condition concerning establishment and conduct in good faith;
- the general condition concerning the minimum number of members;
- the general condition that alcohol is not supplied, or intended to be supplied, to members on the premises other than by or on behalf of the club; and
- the three additional conditions set out on page 10.

For these purposes, "miners' welfare institute" means an association organised for the social well-being and recreation of persons employed in or about coal mines. Such an institute is "relevant" if it satisfies one of the following conditions:
- it is managed by a committee or board, at least two thirds of which consists of persons appointed or nominated by coal industry operators and by organisations representing persons employed in or about coal mines; or
- where appointment of board members as above is not practicable or appropriate, at least two-thirds of the committee or board must consist of persons employed, or formerly employed, in or about coal mines and persons appointed by the Coal Industry Social Welfare Organisation or a successor

organisation; or
- the premises of the institute are held on trusts to which section 2 of the Recreational Charities Act 1958 applies, that is mining industry trusts declared before 17 December 1957 relating to property held for the purposes of social welfare activities (such as the maintenance or improvement of health, social well-being, recreation or living conditions) as defined in the Miners' Welfare Act 1952.

7. Club Ceasing to be Qualified

Section 90 of the Licensing Act deals with the withdrawal of its certificate if a club ceases to be a qualifying club. A licensing authority may withdraw a club premises certificates if it appears that the relevant club no longer satisfies the qualifying conditions described above. If an authority intends to withdraw a certificate, it must first give notice of its intention. A club may cease to be a qualifying club in relation to a particular qualifying activity only. In such a case, the notice given by the authority to the club must state that the certificate is to be withdrawn in respect of that particular activity.

If the only reason the club ceases to be qualified is that the number of members has fallen below twenty-five, the notice withdrawing the certificate must state that the withdrawal will not take effect for three months, and will not taken effect at all if, at the end of the three months, the number of members has been restored to the minimum twenty-five.

In some instances, although a licensing authority has cause to suspect that a club no longer qualifies for the certificate it holds, the suspicion alone is not sufficient to warrant the service of a notice of withdrawal. The Act anticipates this difficulty and makes provision for the licensing authority to obtain authorisation to enter the club premises and search them for evidence that might confirm the suspicion. The licensing authority must apply to a magistrate. If the magistrate is satisfied, by evidence given on oath, that there are reasonable grounds for believing:
- that a club holding a club premises certificate does not satisfy the conditions for being a qualifying club in relation to a qualifying club activity to which the certificate relates; and
- that evidence of that fact is to be obtained at the premises to

which the certificate relates,
the magistrate may issue a warrant. The warrant authorises a constable to enter the premises, by force if necessary, at any time within one month from the date the warrant is issued, and search the premises. A person who enters premises under the authority of such a warrant may seize and remove any documents relating to the business of the club in question.

The Act is silent as to who is to be expected to give the sworn evidence in support of an application for a warrant to enter and search club premises. It seems that the evidence may be given by an officer of the authority which suspects that the club has ceased to qualify for the certificate it holds, or by the constable who wishes to enter and search the club premises for evidence to support such a suspicion.

Chapter 3

Transitional Applications

1. Introduction

To deal with the transitional period leading up to the coming into full force of the Licensing Act 2003, some arrangement had to be made in relation to the many thousands of members' clubs already operating on the authority of club registration certificates granted under the Licensing Act of 1964. Many hoped that there would be a provision in the new Act to the effect that any existing club registration certificate would be deemed to be a club premises certificate for the purposes of the new regime, but Parliament decided against such a provision. Consequently, it is necessary for every registered club to apply for the conversion of its existing club registration certificate, and any ancillary orders that may attach to it, into a premises certificate pursuant to the new Act. The 2003 Act provides for these applications for conversion. The procedures are set out in Schedule 8 to the Act, and clubs are dealt with specifically in Part 2 of that schedule.

Transitional applications may be submitted at any time during the transitional period of six months which began on "the first appointed day", that is, 7 February 2005. The transitional procedures are set out in the following paragraphs.

2. Application for Conversion of Certificate

An application for the conversion of a club registration certificate must be in the specified form, reproduced in Appendix A. Much of the form concerns the club operating schedule; the information to be given under this heading is as follows:

- a general description of the club premises – their situation and

layout, and any other information relevant to the licensing objectives;
- the qualifying club activities authorised by the existing certificate, including the type(s) of entertainment, if any, provided by the club;
- any limitations on the hours during which the club is permitted to conduct club qualifying activities, including the supply of alcohol, under its existing certificate or other authorisations (for more on licensing hours, see Chapter 14);
- any conditions subject to which the existing certificate was granted, with specific reference to the licensing objectives (see page 3).

The application must be accompanied by the "relevant documents" and the specified fee. The fee payable is on a scale between £100 and £635, depending on the non-domestic rateable value of the premises; see Appendix B for details.

The "relevant documents" are:
- the existing club registration certificate(s), or certified copy/ies;
- a plan of the premises to which the existing certificate relates (in the specified form – see below); and
- a copy of the club's rules (see the Licensing Act 2003 (Transitional Provisions) Order 2005, Statutory Instrument 2005 No. 40).

Any ancillary certificates and orders relating to the club's registration, such as a supper hour certificate or special hours order, should also accompany the application if their effect is to be reproduced in the new certificate.

A "certified copy" of a document is a copy document certified to be a true copy by, most commonly, the chief executive of the licensing justices for the district in which the premises are situated, or a solicitor or notary.

The Licensing Act 2003 (Transitional Provisions) Order 2005 contains requirements concerning the plan of the premises which is to accompany the application. Unless the licensing authority agrees in writing, following a request by the applicant, that an alternative scale plan is acceptable, the plan should be drawn on the standard scale of 1:100. The plan must show:
- the extent of the boundary of the building, if relevant, and any external and internal walls of the building and, if different, the

perimeter of the premises;
- the location of points of access to and egress from the premises;
- if different from the above, the location of escape routes from the premises;
- where the premises are used for more than one existing qualifying club activity, the area within the premises used for each activity;
- where an existing qualifying club activity relates to the supply of alcohol, the location(s) on the premises used for the consumption of alcohol;
- fixed structures (including furniture) or similar objects temporarily in a fixed location (but not furniture) which may impact on the ability of individuals on the premises to use exits or escape routes without impediment;
- where the premises include a stage or raised area, the location and height of each stage or raised area relative to the floor;
- where the premises include any steps, stairs, elevators or lifts, their location;
- where the premises include any room(s) containing public conveniences, the location of the room(s);
- the location and type of any fire safety equipment and any other safety equipment; and
- the location of any kitchen.

The plan may include a legend of symbols illustrating the above items on the plan.

3. The Role of the Police

A person applying to convert a club registration certificate to a club premises certificate must give a copy of the application and all accompanying documents to the chief officer of police for the police area or areas in which the relevant premises are situated. The notice must be given not less than forty-eight hours after the application is made. The legislation does not allow licensing authorities any discretion in relation to application procedures. If the statutory requirements are not followed to the letter, the authority is not able to consider the application.

If, when the application is made, there is an appeal pending against a decision to revoke the existing club certificate or to reject an application for its renewal, and the chief officer of police is satisfied that converting the existing licence under these transitional provisions would undermine the crime prevention objective (one of the licensing objectives described on page 3), he must give notice to that effect to the relevant licensing authority and the applicant.

Similarly, if a chief officer who has received notice of an application to convert a club registration certificate is satisfied that, because of a material change in circumstances since the relevant time, converting the existing club certificate would undermine the crime prevention objective, he must give notice to that effect to the licensing authority and the applicant. "The relevant time" here means the time when the existing certificate was granted or last renewed. In either case, the chief officer must give the required notice within twenty-eight days of the day on which he received a copy of the application. Notices given after that time are not valid.

It is important to understand that the only ground on which the police can object to a transitional application is that they believe that granting it would undermine the crime prevention objective. Nor is there any right for anyone other than the police to make representations concerning an application for conversion.

4.   Determining an Application for Conversion

The requirements described here apply when an application for the conversion of an existing registration certificate has been submitted in accordance with the procedure set out above. Unless the police have served a notice as described above, and that notice has not been withdrawn, the licensing authority *must* grant the application. But if a notice has been given by the police, the authority must hold a hearing to consider it, unless the chief officer of police and the applicant agree that a hearing is unnecessary. The authority must consider the notice at the hearing and, if it considers it necessary for the promotion of the crime prevention objective, it must reject the application. Otherwise, the application should be granted.

For the procedure at hearings, see page 35.

It is difficult to think of many circumstances in which the police and the applicant would agree that a hearing is not necessary. Perhaps if the applicant were to give assurances to the chief officer of police which satisfied his concerns in relation to the crime prevention objective, the police would be prepared to withdraw the notice. The schedule makes clear, however, that no hearing is required if the notice is withdrawn; it would not be a question of the authority's being relieved of its obligation to hold a hearing by virtue of the consensus reached by the chief officer and the applicant.

If there is to be a hearing, the authority has two months in which to determine the application to convert the club premises certificate. The two months begin on the day the application is received by the authority. If, by the end of that period, the application has not been determined then, as a general rule, it is to be treated as having been granted by the authority. Exceptionally, the application is not to be granted or treated as granted if the existing registration certificate has ceased to have effect at the time the application is to be determined, or at the end of the two month period allowed for a hearing to be held.

Where the licensing authority is required to hold a hearing to determine the application, it must determine the application itself; it may not delegate the decision to an officer of the authority.

It will be interesting to see how many applications are determined within the period allowed by the statute. Much will depend on the frequency with which the police feel it necessary to give notices. It is likely that most unopposed transitional applications will be dealt with by officers of the licensing authority using their delegated powers. Since many authorities have found it difficult to engage sufficient experienced staff, it remains to be seen how many applications will go through by default.

5. The Secretary of State's Guidance

Advice in relation to the submission and determination of applications during the transitional period is to be found in paragraph 13 of the Secretary of State's Guidance Document issued under section 182 of the Licensing Act 2003. The status of the guidance is a little confusing. It is clear that it does not have the force of law and that those to whom it is addressed are not obliged to act upon it. However, in carrying out their functions under the Act, licensing authorities are required to "have regard" to such guidance. The Secretary of State expresses the view that the guidance is important for consistency, particularly where licensing authority boundaries meet.

No doubt the status of the Guidance Document will be tested in the High Court at an early date. It is arguable that an application for judicial review would be appropriate if it appears that a licensing authority has not had sufficient regard to the Guidance Document when carrying out any of its function under the Act.

The following extracts from the Guidance Document may be of some importance when transitional applications are being processed.

"13.2 . . . In carrying out any licensing function . . ., a licensing authority must have regard to both this Guidance and its own statement of licensing policy.

13.3 The licensing authority's aim should be to ensure as smooth, efficient and rapid a transition as possible . . .

13.4 The transitional period will be a difficult and demanding period for licensing authorities, responsible authorities and for applicants. It is therefore important that, so far as possible, licensing authorities, responsible authorities and representatives of the holders of existing . . . registration certificates should work together to ensure a smooth transition both before and from the first appointed day at the start of the transitional period. This might include, for example, agreeing arrangements with many of the businesses [clubs] affected for staggering applications throughout the first six months of the transitional period to avoid gluts of applications made on the same day".

6. Notification of Determination and Issue of New Certificate

When an application for a new certificate is granted, the relevant licensing authority must give notice of the grant, forthwith, to the applicant, and issue a new certificate in respect of the premises, and a summary of the certificate. See Appendix A for the form of the certificate and summary.

If the application is rejected, the authority must, forthwith, give the applicant a notice to that effect. The notice must contain a statement of the authority's reasons for the decision to reject the application. The authority is also under a duty to give a copy of any such notice to the chief officer of police for the area (or areas) in which the premises are situated.

7.   The New Certificate

The new certificate is to be treated as if it were a club premises certificate. It takes effect on the "second appointed day". At the time of writing, the second appointed day has not been specified, but it is expected to be in November 2005. Until the second appointed day, the certificate granted under the 1964 Act still has effect.

The new certificate must authorise the use of the premises for the existing qualifying club activities. As the certificate is to be treated as a club premises certificate, sections 73 (relating to the supply of alcohol for consumption off the premises), 74 (relating to mandatory conditions in respect of films) and 75 (relating to prohibited conditions in respect of associate members their guests) apply to it. See pages 31–32 for details of these conditions.

The new certificate must also be subject to such conditions as have the effect of reproducing those attaching to the existing certificate at the time the application is granted. It must also be granted subject to conditions that reproduce the effect of any restrictions imposed on the use of the premises for the existing qualifying club activities by any enactment.

There is, however, no provision requiring or allowing the authority to grant the new certificate for a limited period. The certificate is therefore of indefinite duration unless surrendered or withdrawn, and there is no need to apply for renewal.

8.   Variation of Certificate

It is possible to apply for the variation of a certificate even before the application to convert it has been determined. While the application for conversion is pending, or simultaneously with the application for conversion, an application for variation may be made in accordance with section 84 of the 2003 Act. For the purposes of such an application the applicant is treated as if he were the holder of the new certificate. However, even though the two applications may be made simultaneously, the licensing authority may not deal with the application for variation until the application for conversion has been granted.

The prescribed form of application for variation is set out in Appendix A and is discussed in Chapter 6.

An application for variation made in this way is to be treated as having been rejected at the end of a period of two months, beginning with the day it was received by the licensing authority, if it has not been determined within that period.

A problem arises where a club submits an application for conversion together with an application for variation, but the licensing authority does not deal with the application for conversion within the prescribed time limit; the authority will not then be in a position to consider the application for variation. In effect, both applications are dealt with by default: the application for conversion is deemed to be granted, but the application for variation is deemed to be rejected. Should such a situation occur, the applicant will be left with little choice but to appeal against the deemed rejection to the magistrates' court.

9. Revocation of Existing Club Certificate

Where a licensing authority has granted a new certificate as described above, but the existing club certificate is revoked before the second appointed day, the new certificate lapses. The new certificate also lapses if an appeal against a decision to revoke the old certificate, which was pending immediately before the second appointed day, is dismissed or abandoned.

The effect of these provisions is to bring to an end any new certificate granted pursuant to the transitional provisions if the original certificate is revoked before the second appointed day. This is because a new certificate does not become effective until the second appointed day and then comes into effect only if the certificate on which it was based remains in force.

10. Appeals

Should a licensing authority reject an application for the conversion of an existing club certificate, the applicant may appeal against the rejection. Where an application for conversion is granted, any chief officer of police who gave a notice in respect of the application (see pages 16–17) may appeal against the grant of the certificate, as long as the notice had not been withdrawn before the decision to grant the application was made.

Details of the provisions concerning appeals are to be found in section 181 of the Act, and Schedule 5, Part 2.

11. False Statements

It is an offence for a person knowingly or recklessly to make a false statement in or in connection with an application for the conversion of an existing club premises certificate. A person is treated as making a false statement if he produces, furnishes, signs or otherwise makes use of a document that contains a false statement. The maximum penalty for this offence is a fine not exceeding £5,000.

These provisions seem to be worded in such a way that a legal representative, making an application on behalf of a client, could be guilty of the offence if he furnishes or signs a document that transpires to contain a false statement. Both solicitors and their clients are wise to verify all information before signing and submitting an application.

12. Checklist

- Application to the licensing authority, together with:
    - the appropriate scale fee,
    - the existing club registration certificate or a certified copy,
    - any ancillary certificates or orders;
    - a plan of the club premises, and
    - a copy of the club rules.
- Copy of all documents to be sent to the chief officer of police.

Chapter 4

Application for New Club Premises Certificate

1.   Introduction

During the transitional period which started on 7 February 2005, any group wishing to have the benefit of members' club registration for the first time must apply to the magistrates' court that has jurisdiction over the area in which the club premises are situated, for a club registration certificate, in accordance with the provisions of the Licensing Act 1964.

After the second appointed day (at the time of going to press, the date of the second appointed day has not been fixed, but it is expected to be in November 2005), the procedures under the Licensing Act 1964 are no longer available and an application for a club premises certificate must be submitted to the local authority for the area in which the premises are situated. Part 4 of the Licensing Act 2003 deals with such applications, and with other matters relating to club premises certificates.

The form of application and certain other matters – the fees payable, notices to be given, and requirements concerning the advertisement of applications, are to be found in regulations made by the Secretary of State under powers granted by the Act.

2.   The Application

A club may apply for a certificate for any premises that are occupied by, and habitually used for the purposes of, the club. The application must be made to the relevant licensing authority.

Form of Declaration

When the application is submitted, the club must make a declaration, in writing, that it is a qualifying club (see page 9 *et seq)*. The declaration must be sent to the licensing authority. It must be in the form prescribed in the Licensing Act 2003 (Premises Licences and Club Premises Certificates) Regulations 2005, Statutory Instrument 2005 No. 42. The form is reproduced in Appendix A.

Form of Application

The form of application is also prescribed by the Licensing (Premises Licences and Club Premises Certificates) Regulations 2005, and is set out in Appendix A. The first part of the form calls for the following information:

- the name and address of the club;
- the name and address of the club secretary, or person performing the duties of a club secretary;
- confirmation that the premises are occupied and habitually used by the club;
- the date from which the applicant wishes the certificate to start, and, if it is to be valid for a limited time only, the date on which it is to end;
- a general description of the club;
- the number of persons likely to be on the premises at any one time, if more than 5,000.

In the next part of the form, the club's operating schedule is to be set out. It includes:

- the regulated entertainments, if any, which are to provided by the club;
- the entertainment facilities, if any, which are to be provided by the club;
- whether or not the club will supply alcohol to, or to the order of, members; if so, whether the supply will be for consumption on or off the premises or both; standard and non-standard times for the supply; and any seasonal variations;
- the hours during which the club premises are to be open to members and guests, including any seasonal variations and non-standard hours. For more about licensing hours, see Chapter 14;
- any adult entertainment or services, activities or other matters that may give rise to concerns in respect of children. The examples of such matters given in the notes to the form are nudity or semi-nudity, films for restricted age groups and the

presence of gambling machines;
- the steps the club will take to promote the licensing objectives (see also pages 30–31, concerning risk assessments).

The regulated entertainments which may be provided are:
- a performance of a play;
- an exhibition of a film;
- an indoor sporting event;
- a boxing or wrestling entertainment;
- a performance of live music;
- any playing of recorded music;
- a performance of dance;
- live music, recorded music or dance which takes place in the presence of an audience and is provided wholly or partly to entertain that audience.

The entertainment facilities which the club may wish to supply are:
- making music;
- dancing; and
- other similar entertainment.

A club which includes any of the above entertainments or entertainment facilities in its operating schedule must give further details, including whether or not the entertainment will take place indoors or outdoors; timings; and seasonal variations.

The fee payable on making the application for a certificate is on a scale between £100 and £635, depending on the non-domestic rateable value of the premises; see Appendix B for details.

The application must be accompanied by a plan of the relevant premises in the prescribed form (see below), a copy of the club rules, and the declaration that the club is a qualifying club. The licensing authority may wish to refer to the rules to satisfy itself that the club is a qualifying club and that its club operating schedule is not inconsistent with its rules. The requirement to submit a copy of the rules is not overridden by the requirement to submit a declaration as to the qualifying status of the club; both must accompany the application.

Plans

The Licensing (Premises Licences and Club Premises Certificates) Regulations 2005 (above) prescribe the form which the plans must take. Plans must be drawn to the standard scale of 1:100, unless the relevant licensing authority has notified the applicant, in writing, that it will accept another scale.

The plan must show:

- the extent of the boundary of the building, if relevant, and any external and internal walls, and, if different, the perimeter of the premises;
- the location of points of access to and egress from the premises;
- if different, the location of escape routes from the premises;
- where the premises are to be used for more than one qualifying activity, the area to be used for each;
- where the supply of alcohol for consumption on the premises is to take place, the location(s) on the premises where alcohol will be consumed;
- fixed structures, including furniture, or similar objects temporarily in a fixed location, which may affect the ability of individuals on the premises to use exits or escape routes without impediment;
- the location and height of any stage or raised area relative to the floor;
- where the premises include any steps, stairs, elevators or lifts, their location;
- where the premises include any room(s) containing public conveniences, the location of the room(s);
- the location and type of any fire safety and any other safety equipment including, if applicable, marine safety equipment; and
- the location of any kitchen(s).

Plans may include a legend that enables the symbols on them to be understood.

Advertisements

The Licensing (Premises Licences and Club Premises Certificates) Regulations also contain requirements to advertise applications for club premises certificates. An applicant for a club premises certificate must advertise the application:

- by displaying a notice containing certain information (see below). The notice must be displayed prominently, at or on the premises to which the application relates, where it can conveniently be read from outside the premises. It must be of a size equal to or larger than A4, printed legibly in a font size

27

equal to or larger than 16, on pale blue paper. Multiple copies of the notice must be displayed on premises covering an area of more than 50 metres square. The notice must be displayed for a continuous period of not less than twenty-eight consecutive days, starting on the day following the day the application is given to the relevant licensing authority; and
• by publishing a notice in a local newspaper or, if there is none, in a local newsletter, circular or similar document circulating in the vicinity of the premises, again containing certain information (see below). The notice must be published on at least one occasion during the period of ten working days starting on the day after the application to the licensing authority.

The wording of the requirement to publish a notice in the press is interesting. Earlier legislation required press advertisements to be placed in a newspaper circulating in the district. *R v Westminster Betting Licensing Committee, ex parte Peabody Donation Fund Governors* was authority for the view that the newspaper in question did not have to be a local paper, as long as it circulated in the relevant district. In the new regulations the words used suggest that publication in a national newspaper will not do, even though it may circulate in the relevant area.

The information which must be included in both the notice displayed on the premises and in the newspaper advertisement is:
• the club qualifying activities which it is proposed to carry on from the premises;
• the name of the club;
• the postal address of the club premises, or if there is no postal address, a description of the premises sufficient to enable the location and extent of the premises to be identified;
• the postal address and, where applicable, the worldwide web address where the register of the relevant licensing authority is kept, and where and when the record of the application may be inspected;
• the date by which an interested party or responsible authority may make representations to the relevant licensing authority;
• a statement that representations should be made in writing; and
• a statement that it is an offence knowingly or recklessly to make a false statement in connection with an application, and

the maximum fine to which a person is liable on summary conviction for the offence.

The requirement to advertise applications ensures that any interested persons have the opportunity to make any representations they wish to make concerning an application.

Notice to Responsible Authorities

An applicant must also give a copy of the application, and of all the accompanying documents, to all "responsible authorities". This must be done on the day the application is given to the relevant licensing authority.

"Responsible authorities" are:

- the chief officer of police for the area in which the premises are situated;
- the fire authority;
- the health and safety at work inspectorate;
- the local planning authority;
- the environmental health authority;
- any body having responsibilities for the protection of children from harm, or recognised by the licensing authority as competent to advise on such matters;
- any licensing authority other than the relevant authority; and
- in relation to a vessel, a navigation authority, and certain other bodies.

3. Determination of the Application

Generally, when a licensing authority receives an application for a club premises certificate and the authority is satisfied that the applicant has complied with the application procedures described above, it must grant the application. The obligation to grant is subject only to the proviso that the authority may impose upon the certificate any conditions that are considered to be consistent with the operating schedule submitted as part of the application. The authority must also, if appropriate, impose a mandatory condition concerning the exhibition of films (see page 32).

If relevant representations (see below) are made, however, the authority must hold a hearing to consider them, unless the authority, the applicant and each person who has made representation agree that a hearing is unnecessary. Having had regard to the representations, the authority must then take such steps, if any, as it considers necessary for the promotion of the licensing objectives. The steps that an authority may take for the promotion of licensing objectives are:

- to grant the certificate subject to modifications to the conditions attaching to it. Conditions are regarded as modified if any of them is altered or omitted, or any new condition is added;
- to include in the certificate a mandatory condition concerning the exhibition of films;
- to exclude from the scope of the certificate any qualifying club activities to which the application relates; or
- to reject the application.

The Licensing Act 2003 prohibits the inclusion, in a club premises certificate, of authority for off-sales unless there is also a provision for consumption on the premises; any conditions attached to the certificate must be consistent with this prohibition.

A licensing authority may grant a certificate subject to different conditions in respect of different parts of the club premises or in respect of different qualifying activities. Conditions may, therefore, be imposed in relation to a function room that do not apply to a members' bar and *vice versa*. Similarly, a condition may restrict the provision of late night entertainment though it is of no relevance to the supply of alcohol generally.

The Guidance Document published by the Secretary of State includes a section on conditions attached to club premises certificates. The Guidance emphasises several principles, including the following:

"7.1 . . . Conditions may only be imposed on . . . certificates where they are necessary for the promotion of one or more of the four licensing objectives [see page 3]. Conditions may not be imposed on . . . certificates for other purposes. . .

7.4 The conditions that are necessary for the promotion of the licensing objectives should emerge initially from a prospective . . . certificate holder's risk assessment which should be undertaken by . . . clubs before making their application for a . . . club premises certificate. This would be translated into the steps recorded in the . . . club operating schedule that it is proposed to take to promote the licensing objectives. . . Where the responsible authorities and interested parties do not raise any representations about the application made to the licensing authority, it is the duty of the authority to grant the . . . certificate subject only to conditions that are consistent with the . . . club operating schedule and any mandatory conditions prescribed in the 2003 Act itself.

7.5 The licensing authority may not therefore impose any conditions unless its discretion has been engaged following the making of relevant representations and it has been satisfied at a hearing of the necessity to impose conditions due to the representations raised. It may then only impose such conditions as are necessary to promote the licensing objectives arising out of the consideration of the representations."

For more on risk assessments, see Chapter 16.

This guidance makes clear that a licensing authority ought not to impose conditions on club premises certificates because of the preferences of its members or of the electorate. It also makes clear that if representations are made in respect of one licensing objective only, for example, the protection of children, the licensing authority may not impose conditions designed to uphold another of the licensing objectives – the public safety objective, say.

Clubs wishing to apply for a club premises certificate would be well advised to commission or otherwise carry out a risk assessment to determine the extent to which, if at all, the proposed qualifying activities would put the four licensing objectives at risk, before completing the club operating schedule to be submitted with the application. The steps being taken to address those risks can then be included in the schedule.

4.   Off-sales

Under the 1964 Licensing Act, registered clubs were authorised to supply intoxicating liquor to members for consumption off the club premises. They were not authorised to supply guests with intoxicants for that purpose. The Act of 2003 introduces the concept of a certificate that specifically authorises off-sales. A club premises certificate may not, however, authorise the supply of alcohol for consumption off the premises unless it also authorises the supply of alcohol to members for consumption on those premises.

In addition, any certificate that authorises supply for consumption off the premises must include the following conditions:

- such supply may be made only when the premises are open for the purpose of supplying members with alcohol for consumption on the premises;
- the alcohol supplied for consumption off the premises must be in sealed containers; and
- the supply in question must be made to a member of the club in person.

It seems, therefore, that where the appropriate certificate is held, a member could purchase alcohol while the club is open to members, even though it is intended that the alcohol will be consumed by a guest off the premises.

5. Mandatory Condition: Films

Where a club premises certificate authorises the exhibition of films, it must include a condition that the admission of children is to be restricted.

Where the certificate specifies the British Board of Film Classification, the admission of children must be restricted in accordance with its recommendations, unless the licensing authority has given notice to the club that its own recommendations are to be applied. Where such a notice has been given, or where no classification body is specified in the certificate, the restrictions recommended by the licensing authority must be observed.

For these purposes "children" means persons under the age of eighteen.

6. Prohibited Conditions

Associate Members and Guests

If the rules of a club provide for the sale of alcohol on behalf of the club to associate members or their guests, no condition may be imposed upon the premises certificate that would have the effect of preventing such sales from taking place.

Similarly, if the rules of a club allow for the provision of regulated entertainment on club premises, by or on behalf of the club and for the benefit of associate members or their guests, no condition may be attached to the premises certificate that would negate that rule.

Plays

Generally, if a club premises certificate authorises the performance of plays on the premises, the licensing authority may not attach a condition which relates to the nature of the plays which may be performed or the manner in which they are performed. The authority is not, however, prevented from attaching any condition that it considers necessary on the grounds of public safety.

An example of when it may be appropriate for a licensing authority to attach a condition which would restrict the nature of plays or the manner in which they may be performed might be where the size of the stage or other equipment are such that the use of certain effects would cause danger.

7. Representations

Those Who May Make Representations

An application submitted under the 2003 Act may give rise to representations as to whether or not it should be granted. To facilitate proper decisions as to whether or not representations are "relevant", the Act provides that representations may be made only by "authorised persons", "interested parties" and "responsible authorities". These are defined in section 69 of the Act.

An authorised person includes:
- a licensing officer of the local licensing authority;
- a fire inspector;
- a health and safety inspector; and
- an environmental health officer.

An interested party is:
- a person living in the vicinity of the premises for which the certificate is sought, or a body, such as a residents' association, that represents such persons;
- a person involved in a business in the vicinity of the premises, or a body that represents such persons (such as a local chamber of commerce).

Responsible authorities include:
- the police;
- the fire authority;
- the health and safety at work inspectorate;
- the planning authority;
- the environmental health authority;

- bodies concerned with the protection of children from harm, which are recognised by the licensing authority as competent to advise it on such matters;
- a licensing authority other than the one in whose area part of the premises is situated; and
- in relation to a vessel, a navigation authority, the Environment Agency, the British Waterways Board, the Secretary of State, and any other person prescribed for the purpose.

Relevant Representations

Licensing authorities are obliged to take account of "relevant" representations only. To be regarded as relevant, representations must relate to the likely effect of granting the application on the promotion of the licensing objectives. For example, the police may make a representation that, having regard to the location of the club premises, granting the certificate with the hours applied for would undermine the objective of preventing public nuisance; or the fire authority may make a representation that the use of the club premises for a particular activity, having regard to the numbers likely to attend, would undermine the public safety objective.

Representations must also be made within the time limits set down and must not have been withdrawn.

An authority may reject a representation on the ground that it is vexatious or frivolous, but if it does so, it must give notice of that decision to the person who submitted the representation and state why it has been held to be vexatious or frivolous. If a representation is a repeat of one that was submitted and considered by the authority in relation to a previous application in respect of the club premises, it may be treated as a frivolous representation and not relevant.

In the Guidance Document issued in accordance with section 182 of the Act, the Secretary of State has suggested that all decisions on whether a representation is to be considered frivolous or vexatious should be delegated to officers of the licensing authority, rather than being dealt with by the licensing committee itself. This advice appears a little strange since such a decision can be the subject of an appeal to the magistrates' court. It is clearly a judicial decision and one might expect officers to be wary of making it, especially where the application in question is for a licence or certificate. On an application for variation or review of a certificate, an officer may be more ready to make such a decision, especially if the licensing committee heard a similar representation in relation to the original grant and rejected it.

Right of Audience

Statutory regulations (The Licensing Act 2003 (Hearings) Regulations 2005, Statutory Instrument 2005 No. 78) govern the way hearings of licensing matters by licensing authorities are to be run. Generally, any party to an application that is to be heard before a licensing committee may attend the hearing and may be assisted or represented by any person, whether or not that person is legally qualified. This is a departure from the position under earlier legislation. Until now, only qualified persons could represent applicants unless specific authorisation to act had been given to an unqualified person by the licensing committee.

The regulations do, however, contain provisions that may limit the general right to be present at a hearing and to be represented before the committee. The regulations require hearings to be held in a public place, but they also provide that the licensing authority may exclude the public from all or part of the hearing where it considers that the public interest in doing so outweighs the public interest in a hearing in public. In this respect, a party or person assisting or representing a party may be treated as a member of the public.

Because of the implications of a decision to exclude from a hearing any legal representative assisting an applicant, it is expected that the power to exclude will be used only very rarely. Such an exclusion would be likely to raise the question of a breach of Article 7 of the European Convention on Human Rights – the right to a fair hearing.

Less controversial, perhaps, is the licensing authority's power under the regulations to require disruptive persons to leave the hearing and to refuse to let them return, or to let them return only if they comply with any conditions imposed by the authority.

8. The Grant or Rejection of the Application

When a licensing authority grants an application for a club premises certificate, it must give notice of the grant, forthwith, to:
- the applicant;
- any person who made a relevant representation; and
- the chief officer of police for the area in which the premises

are situated.

The authority must also issue the club with a premises certificate and a summary of it (see Appendix A). If relevant representations were made, the notification of grant must include the authority's reasons for its decision and any steps it has taken to promote the licensing objectives. The licensing authority must give notice to the same people of any decision to reject an application for a club premises certificate. Again, the notice given must state the authority's reasons for rejecting the application.

9. The Form of the Certificate and Summary

Club premises certificates and summaries of them must be in the form prescribed in regulations (see Appendix A). In particular, a club premises certificate must:

- specify the name of the club and its relevant registered address;
- specify the address of the premises to which the certificate relates;
- include a plan of the club premises;
- specify the qualifying club activities for which the premises may be used; and
- specify any conditions to which the certificate is subject.

"Relevant registered address" is the address given by the holder of the certificate as the one to be recorded in the licensing authority's records.

10. Checklist

- Application (including the club operating schedule) to the licensing authority, together with:
  - a plan of the premises,
  - a declaration by the club as to its qualifying status,
  - a copy of the club rules, and
  - the appropriate fee;
- notice to be given to the responsible authorities; and
- the application is to be advertised as prescribed.

11. Appeals

A club that is aggrieved by a decision made by the licensing authority may appeal against that decision. Initially, appeals are to the local magistrates' court. If the appellant club is still unhappy with the decision once the magistrates have adjudicated, a further appeal to the Crown Court is possible. Generally, appeals will be lodged on the basis that the decision reached was not justified, having regard to the evidence produced by the club and by any persons who, or authorities which, opposed the application.

Where the grievance is that the proper procedures were not followed, or that the decision reached was contrary to law, the proper remedy would be to seek leave from the High Court to make an application for judicial review. Although there may be an unusually high number of applications for judicial review while the new procedures are "bedding in", it is likely that most appeals brought by clubs will be to the magistrates' court.

Part 2 of Schedule 5 to the Licensing Act 2003 makes provision for appeals relating to club premises certificates. It allows for an appeal to be brought where a club is aggrieved by a decision:

- rejecting an application for a club premises certificate;
- to impose conditions on the grant of a club premises certificate;
- to modify the conditions attached to a club premises certificate on an application for variation;
- in connection with an application for the review of a club premises certificate; or
- to withdraw a club premises certificate.

An appeal brought under Schedule 5 should be to the magistrates' court for the area in which the relevant premises are situated. Notice of appeal must be given to the chief executive to the magistrates' court within twenty-one days beginning with the date on which the appellant was notified of the decision appealed against.

A club may also appeal against any decision taken by the licensing authority in relation to a temporary event notice (see Chapter 9) given by an individual on its behalf.

Section 181 of the Licensing Act provides that, when determining an appeal, the magistrates may:

- dismiss the appeal,
- substitute for the decision appealed against any other decision which could have been made by the licensing authority, or

- remit the case to the licensing authority to dispose of it in accordance with the direction of the court.

The magistrates may make such order for costs as it thinks fit.

It is difficult to think of circumstances in which the magistrates would decide to remit a matter to the licensing authority for disposal. Since they have the power to substitute any decision that the authority could have come to for the one that was actually made, there would, generally, seem to be no need to use the power to remit.

Although the magistrates can make such order as to costs as they think fit, they must be mindful of the cases of *R v Totnes Licensing Justices, ex parte Chief Constable of Devon and Cornwall* and *R v Merthyr Tydfil Crown Court ex parte Chief Constable of Dyfed Powys Police*. These cases are authority for the view that costs should not be ordered against the police if, in objecting to an application or resisting an appeal, they have simply been carrying out their obligations under the licensing legislation. But if the magistrates are satisfied that the police intervened unreasonably or maliciously, an order for payment of costs would be appropriate.

Chapter 5

The Club Premises Certificates

1. Theft or Loss

Section 79 of the Licensing Act 2003 deals with the theft or loss of a club premises certificate or summary. It provides that if a club premises certificate, or a summary of one, is stolen, lost, damaged or destroyed, the club may apply to the relevant licensing authority for a copy. The licensing authority may charge a fee, currently £10.50, for providing a copy.

When a licensing authority receives an application for a copy document, it must provide a copy if it is satisfied that the original has been lost, stolen, damaged or destroyed; and, in the case of theft or loss, that the club has reported the matter to the police. The copy provided must be certified to be a true copy by the authority. It must be a copy of the original document in the form in which it existed immediately before it was lost, stolen, damaged or destroyed. A certified copy of a certificate or summary has the same effect as the original document for the purposes of the legislation.

2. Duration

Section 80 of the 2003 Act concerns the period of validity of a club premises certificate. Once granted, such a certificate has effect until such time as it is withdrawn by the licensing authority (see page 41), or lapses as a result of being surrendered by the club (see below). A certificate does not have effect during any period when it is suspended (see pages 46–47).

There is no requirement to apply for periodic renewal.

If a club ceases to be qualified to hold a club premises

certificate, the licensing authority may withdraw it; see page 41.

3.   Surrender
If a club decides that it wishes to surrender its club premises certificate it may give notice to that effect to the licensing authority. The notice must be accompanied by the club premises certificate or, if that is not practicable, by a statement of the reasons for the failure to produce it. The certificate lapses when the authority receives the notice. (Licensing Act 2003, section 81.)

4.   Changes of Name, Rules, Address
From time to time a club may wish to change its name or its address, or make alterations to its rules. Sections 82 and 83 of the Licensing Act concern such matters. A club is at liberty to make changes of this kind without having to apply to the licensing authority, but the club secretary must notify the licensing authority of any such changes. This duty applies to any club that holds a club premises certificate, or any club that has made an application for a certificate which has still to be determined by the authority. The fee payable on making such a notification is currently £10.50.

The notice must be accompanied by the club premises certificate or, if that is not practicable, by a statement of the reasons why it cannot be produced.

When an authority receives a notice of change of name or of club rules, it must amend the premises certificate accordingly. The obligation to amend does not, however, apply to any notification that would have the effect of changing the club premises. If a club wishes to change its premises it must apply to vary its premises certificate (see Chapter 6).

Club secretaries must give notice of any change of name or club rules within twenty-eight days of the day on which the change is made. Failure to give the notice within the prescribed period is an offence for which the secretary could be fined a sum not exceeding £500.

It is curious that notice of these changes is to be given to the licensing authority only. There is no obligation to inform the chief officer of police, nor is the licensing authority under a duty to tell the police about any change that is made. Problems may well arise where the police are not aware of a change, particularly to club rules. To avoid such difficulties, it would be good practice to advise the police of any changes.

Should there be a change in the club's relevant registered address (see page 36 for the meaning of "relevant registered address"), notice of the change may be given to the relevant licensing authority so that it can change the record in its licensing register. If a club ceases to have authority to use an address that it has used as its relevant registered address, it must give notice of that fact to the licensing authority, as soon as reasonably practicable. The notice must include details of a new address that is to be the club's relevant registered address. A fee (currently £10.50) is payable on making such a notification.

The need to give notice of a change of registered address is likely to arise where there is a change of club officers. For example, if the registered address has been the address of the club secretary, and a different person is elected to that office, the club's authority to use the outgoing secretary's address may come to an end.

A notice of change of registered address must be accompanied by the club premises certificate or, if that is not practicable, a statement of the reasons for the failure to produce it. The licensing authority must amend the club premises certificate upon receipt of notice of a change of relevant registered address.

If a club fails to give notice of a change of registered address, the club secretary commits an offence that may be punished by a fine not exceeding £500.

5. Club No Longer a Qualifying Club
As noted above, a club premises certificate generally has effect until such time as it is withdrawn by the licensing authority. Section 90 concerns the withdrawal of such a certificate by the licensing authority where the club ceases to be a qualifying club.

Where the licensing authority has reason to believe that a club no longer qualifies for a premises certificate in relation to a qualifying activity included in the premises certificate, it must give notice to the club of withdrawal of the certificate, so far as it relates to that activity.

If the failure to satisfy qualifying conditions consists solely of the fact that there are fewer than twenty-five members, the notice of withdrawal must state that it does not take effect until the end of a period of three months following the date of the notice, and that it will not take effect at all if, by the end of that period, the number of members has risen to at least the minimum qualifying number (twenty-five).

Nothing in the Act prevents a licensing authority from giving a further notice of withdrawal, at any time, if it has reason to believe that the club no longer satisfies a qualifying condition.

6.   Warrants of Entry to Obtain Evidence

Where evidence of a failure to satisfy qualifying conditions may be found on club premises, the police may apply for a warrant to search those premises. Where a justice of the peace is satisfied, on information on oath, that a club which holds a premises certificate does not satisfy club qualifying conditions, and that evidence of that fact is to be obtained at the premises to which the certificate relates, the justice of the peace may issue a warrant authorising a constable to enter the premises at any time within one month of the issue of the warrant and to search them. Reasonable force may be used to gain entry, and the constable is authorised to seize and remove any documents relating to the business of the club.

Chapter 6

Variation and Review of Club Premises Certificate

1. Introduction

Occasionally, a club may wish to alter its club premises. If so, it must apply for a variation of the club's premises certificate. A situation may also arise in which an interested party, responsible authority or a member of a club thinks it necessary for the licensing authority to review the premises certificate held by the club. Such eventualities are catered for; the procedures for variation are set out in sections 84 to 86 of the Licensing Act 2003; and for review, in sections 87 to 89.

2. Variation

The Application

If a club wishes to change in any way the premises to which the premises certificate relates, it may apply to the relevant licensing authority for variation of the certificate. The application must be accompanied by the club premises certificate or, if that is not practicable, a statement of the reasons for failing to provide it. The form of application is prescribed by regulations and is reproduced in Appendix A. The form calls for, among other matters, a description of the change contemplated; details of the effect it would have on the club operating schedule; and details of any additional steps to be taken by the club to promote the licensing objectives. The fee payable on making the application is on a scale from £100 to £635, depending on the rateable value of the premises (see Appendix B).

An application for the variation of a club premises certificate must be advertised, and notice given to the responsible authorities, in the same way as for an original application for a certificate. Details of these requirements are set out in Chapter 4 (see pages 27–29).

Determination of the Application

Generally, when a licensing authority receives an application for the variation of a club premises certificate and it is satisfied that the applicant has complied with all the requirements relating to advertisements, it must grant the application. If, however, "relevant representations" are made in respect of the application, the authority must hold a hearing, unless the applicant and each person who has made such representation agree that it is not necessary to do so. For the provisions on representations and hearings, see Chapter 4, pages 34–35.

Where there is a hearing, the authority, having regard to the representations, must take such steps as it considers necessary for the promotion of the licensing objectives. The steps that might be taken are:

- the modification of the conditions of the certificate, by altering or omitting any of them, or by adding any new condition; or
- the rejection of all or part of the application.

Whether granting an unopposed application, or making a determination following representation, the licensing authority must comply with its duties in relation to the mandatory conditions concerning the supply of alcohol for consumption off the premises (see page 31) and in respect of the exhibition of films (see page 32).

Grant or Rejection of Application

When a licensing authority grants an application for the variation of a club premises licence, it must give notice of its decision, forthwith to:

- the applicant;
- any person who made a relevant representation; and
- the chief officer of police for the area in which the premises are situated.

If relevant representations were made, the notice of decision must include the reasons for reaching that decision and any steps taken to promote the licensing objectives. The notice must also specify when the variation is to take effect. The commencement date will be either the date specified in the application for variation or, if that date is before the date on which the applicant is notified of the decision, a later date specified by the licensing authority in the notification.

If an application, or any part of it, is rejected, the authority must also give notice of the decision to the persons listed above. Again, the notice must be given forthwith and it must specify the reasons for the rejection.

The procedure described here may not be used to effect any substantial change to the premises to which the certificate relates. Consequently, if a club wishes to move to completely different premises, it is likely that an application will have to be made for a new premises certificate.

When determining an application for variation, a licensing authority may impose conditions that affect different parts of the premises in respect of different qualifying club activities.

Checklist

- Application to the licensing authority with:
    - the club premises certificate, and
    - the appropriate fee;
- notice to be given to the responsible authorities;
- application to be advertised in the prescribed form and manner.

3.   Review

Interested parties, responsible authorities or members of a club may apply to the licensing authority for the review of a club premises certificate. See page 33 for the meanings of "interested parties" and "responsible authorities". For example, local residents may seek a review of a certificate if they contend that a change in the way the club is run – by introducing more powerful sound reproduction equipment, say – undermines the licensing objective of preventing public nuisance.

The form of application is prescribed by the Licensing (Premises Licences and Club Premises Certificates) Regulations 2005 (Statutory Instrument 2005 No. 42), and is set out in Appendix A. The form calls for a statement of the grounds for review, which must be based on one of the licensing objectives, and for information in support of the application.

The same regulations require that the person making the application must give notice of the application to the club, and to each responsible authority. The notice must be accompanied by a copy of any attachments submitted with the application; and the notice must be given on the same day as the application is given to the licensing authority.

There is no requirement for the applicant to advertise the application to the public; the authority must do this.

The licensing authority may reject a ground of review specified in a notice of application if it is satisfied that:

- it is not relevant to one or more of the licensing objectives; or
- if made by an interested party or a club member, it is frivolous, vexatious or a repetition.

A ground for review is repetitious for these purposes if it is:

- identical or substantially similar to a ground for review specified in a previous application in respect of the same club premises certificate, or to representations considered by the authority before it determined the application for the grant of the certificate; and
- there has not been a reasonable interval of time since that earlier application for review or the grant of the certificate.

If the authority rejects a ground for review of a certificate, it must notify the applicant of the decision. In addition, if the ground was rejected because it was frivolous or vexatious, the notice of rejection must give the authority's reasons for that decision. The authority must give notice of rejection even where only a part of the grounds for review has been rejected. In such circumstances, the notice must make clear that a part of the grounds has been rejected and set out the reasons for the partial rejection.

Determination of the Application

When a licensing authority receives an application for the review of a club premises certificate from a person or body who has complied with the prescribed application procedures, and it has itself complied with specified time limits for the receipt of relevant representations, it must arrange a hearing. For details of the procedure at hearings, see page 35. At the hearing, the authority must consider the application and any relevant representations that is has received. Having had due regard to those representations, the authority must take such steps as it considers necessary for the promotion of the licensing objectives. Such steps may include:

- the modification of any condition attached to the certificate, by altering or omitting a condition or by adding a new one;
- the exclusion of any qualifying club activity from the scope of the certificate;

- the suspension of the certificate for a period not exceeding three months; or
- the withdrawal of the certificate.

The authority must keep in mind the requirement to include in certificates the mandatory conditions concerning the supply of alcohol for consumption off the premises (see page 31) and the exhibition of films (see page 32).

When determining an application, the authority may order that any modification made, or any exclusion of a qualifying activity, is to have effect for a specified period only. That period may not exceed three months.

"Relevant representations" are those that relate to one or more of the licensing objectives and are made by the club, a responsible authority or interested party within the prescribed time limit. A representation is not relevant if it has been withdrawn before the hearing or, in the case of a representation made by an interested party, it has been treated as frivolous or vexatious. Where a representation is considered frivolous or vexatious, the authority must give notice to that effect to the person making the representation, setting out its reasons for that decision.

The licensing authority must give notice of any determination of an application for review and the reasons for the decision reached to:

- the club;
- the applicant;
- any person who made a relevant representation; and
- the chief officer of police for the area in which the premises are situated.

The authority's determination does not have effect until the period allowed for any appeal to be lodged against the decision has elapsed or, where notice of appeal is given, until that appeal is dealt with.

Review Instigated by the Licensing Authority
Where a local authority is both a relevant licensing authority and a responsible authority, it may apply for the review of a club premises certificate in its capacity as a responsible authority; and, in its capacity as a licensing authority, it may determine the application.

It is difficult to see how this will work in practice. If a local authority uses its power to make an application for review and then, as licensing authority, adjudicates upon that application, there would seem to be strong grounds for judicial review on the basis there had been a breach of human rights (the right to a fair hearing) and a breach of the principles of natural justice (the authority acting as judge in its own cause).

Under the 1964 Licensing Act, licensing justices had the power to seek the revocation of a licence of their own volition, but in practice the power was used only rarely. Applications for revocation tended to be made by other statutory authorities. It is to be hoped that the power contained in the Licensing Act 2003 will be used as sparingly.

Checklist

- Application by interested party, responsible authority or member of club to the licensing authority, with the appropriate fee;
- notice of the application to be given to the responsible authorities and to the club.

Chapter 7

Statutory Controls

1. Young Persons

The Licensing Act 2003 changes the law in relation to young persons in club premises. Under the 1964 Licensing Act, the restrictions that applied to public houses did not, in the main, apply to registered members' clubs because they were not "licensed premises". Consequently, the members of such a club were largely free to decide whether young people would be allowed in club premises and whether any other restrictions should apply to them while there. In particular, it was for the members to decide what age limits should apply to the supply of alcohol to, or for consumption by, young people.

The only legal restriction was the prohibition on giving alcohol to a child under the age of five years except in an emergency or on the advice of a registered medical practitioner. The usual advice was that clubs should act in the same way as would a responsible parent. In practice, most clubs imposed their own restrictions, many opting for a minimum age of sixteen years, while others preferred the eighteen years rule imposed in respect of licensed premises.

The new provisions will undoubtedly cause operational problems which clubs have not experienced to date. For example, the fact that many sports clubs have youth sections makes it necessary for them to rethink the way in which their young members are accommodated. This is because the 2003 Act prohibits the presence of persons under the age of sixteen years on club premises while they are being used for the supply of alcohol, unless accompanied by a person who is over the age of eighteen. Some adjustment to accommodation or the times at which certain activities take place may be necessary as a consequence of the changes.

2.   Unaccompanied Children

Section 145 of the Licensing Act prohibits unaccompanied children from being on certain premises. While "relevant club premises" are open for the purpose of supplying alcohol, a child under the age of sixteen is not allowed to be on the premises, unless in the company of a person who has attained the age of eighteen years. The same prohibition applies between the hours of midnight and 5 a.m. Premises are "relevant premises" for these purposes if they are exclusively or primarily used for the supply of alcohol for consumption on the premises, or they are open and being used for the supply of alcohol for consumption on the premises by virtue of a "temporary event notice" (see Chapter 9).

It is not only the officers of the club who commit an offence if an unaccompanied child is allowed on the premises in breach of these prohibitions. Any person who works on the premises, whether paid or unpaid, in a capacity that authorises that person to request the unaccompanied child to leave the premises, also commits the offence. In addition, in the case of club premises, the provision applies to any officer or member of the club present on the premises in a capacity that enables him to make such a request.

There is one important exception to the general rule, which relates to the passage of children from one part of the club premises to another. No offence is committed if the unaccompanied child is on the (relevant) premises solely for the purpose of passing to or from some other place, to or from which there is no other convenient means of access or egress.

A person charged with an offence under these provisions, by reason of that person's own conduct, has a defence if it can be shown that:
- the defendant believed the unaccompanied child was over the age of sixteen or was accompanied by a person over the age of eighteen; and
- either the defendant had taken all reasonable steps to establish the individual's age, or nobody could reasonably have suspected from the individual's appearance that the individual was aged under sixteen or eighteen as the case may be.

A person is treated as having taken all reasonable steps to establish an individual's age if that person asked for evidence of age, and the evidence given would have convinced a reasonable person.

Where a person is charged with the offence by reason of the act or default of another person, for example where the secretary of a club is charged, but it was the club steward who is said to have allowed the unaccompanied young person onto the premises, it is a defence for the person charged to show that he or she exercised all due diligence to avoid committing the offence.

The penalty for an offence of this kind is a fine of up to £1,000.

3. Supply of Alcohol to Children

It is curious that the expression "child" does not mean the same thing throughout the Act of 2003. For the purposes of the prohibition on unaccompanied children above, a "child" is a person who has not attained the age of sixteen, but in relation to the unlawful supply of alcohol, a child is a person who has not attained the age of eighteen. In the latter case, any person who supplied the alcohol or allowed the supply to take place is liable to be charged, and the club itself may also be prosecuted.

Section 146 provides that it is an offence to supply alcohol on behalf of a club:

- to, or to the order of, a member of the club who has not attained the age of eighteen; or
- to the order of an adult member of the club, for consumption by an individual who is aged under eighteen.

A club commits an offence if alcohol is supplied by it or on its behalf:

- to, or to the order of, a member of the club who is under eighteen; or
- on the order of an adult member of the club, to an individual who is under eighteen.

The statutory defences described above are available to persons or clubs charged with an offence under these provisions. The maximum penalty is a fine not exceeding £5,000.

Just as it is offence for a club or a person to supply alcohol to an under-aged child, so it is an offence for any person or club to *allow* the supply of alcohol to a person who has not attained the age of eighteen. Thus, it is an offence for a person knowingly to allow alcohol to be supplied on relevant premises, by or on behalf of the club:

- to or to the order of a member who is under eighteen; or
- on the order of a member of the club, to an individual who is

under eighteen.

The statutory defences mentioned above do not apply to this offence because here the onus is on the prosecution to prove that the defendant *knowingly* allowed the supply. Further, any member or officer of the club who, at the time of the supply, was on the club premises in a capacity that enabled him to prevent that supply, may be guilty of the offence if that member or officer knew that the supply was being or was about to be made.

Again, an offence under these provisions attracts a fine not exceeding £5,000.

4.   Consumption of Alcohol by Children

Section 150 of the Licensing Act 2003 concerns the consumption of alcohol by children. Just as it is an offence for a person to supply alcohol to a child, so it is an offence for a person under the age of eighteen to consume alcohol.

It is also an offence for certain persons knowingly to allow anyone under the age of eighteen to consume alcohol on club premises. Such persons are those who work on the premises, whether paid or unpaid, in a capacity which allows them to prevent such consumption; and any member or officer of the club who is present in a capacity which enables the member or officer to prevent the consumption.

There is, however, an exception in the case of a child over the age of sixteen years who is taking a table meal in the company of adults. The exception applies in relation to a limited range of alcoholic drinks. They are beer, wine and cider. Any such drinks supplied may be consumed by the child only with a meal, and the child must be accompanied throughout the meal by a person who has attained the age of eighteen.

In practice, it is unusual for prosecutions to be brought against young persons who commit this offence even though they are fully aware that what they are doing is unlawful. It is arguable that charging more young people would have a significant impact on under-age drinking. On the other hand, in the case of members' clubs, it may be said that the club is in a much stronger position to know the ages of younger members than a licensee would be in his public house and that, consequently, it should be more difficult for under-age members to commit this offence.

5. Supply of Liqueur Confectionery to Children

It is an offence for a club or any member of a club to supply liqueur confectionery, on behalf of the club, to or for consumption by a member or other individual who is under the age of sixteen. (Once again, the age limit is sixteen, not eighteen.) Section 148 of the Licensing Act 2003 governs this matter.

A person charged with an offence under these provisions may take advantage of the statutory defence set out in the section. Thus, it is a defence for a person who is charged by reason of the defendant's own conduct to prove that the defendant:

- believed that the relevant individual was over sixteen; and
- had either taken all reasonable steps to establish the individual's age, or that nobody could reasonably have suspected from the individual's appearance that the individual was under sixteen.

A person is treated as having taken all reasonable steps to establish an individual's age if the person asked the individual for evidence of age and the evidence produced would have convinced a reasonable person.

Where a person is charged by reason of the act or default of another person, for example where an officer is charged as a result of the default of an employee, it is a defence that the defendant exercised all due diligence to avoid committing the offence.

On conviction, a fine not exceeding £500 may be imposed.

For these purposes, "liqueur confectionery" means confectionery that contains alcohol in a proportion not greater than 0.2 litres of alcohol (of strength not exceeding 57%) per kilogram of confectionery, consisting either of pieces weighing not more than 42 grams or designed to be broken into such pieces for the purpose of consumption.

6. Prohibited Times and Relevant Premises

The provisions of the Licensing Act 2003 relating to the protection of children are not quite as onerous as they may at first appear. Those engaged in the management of members' clubs might find that, on closer examination, they do not present the logistical difficulties that may have been feared. This is because the prohibitions in relation to unaccompanied children apply only at certain times and in respect of certain parts of the premises. It might be possible to make arrangements that allow existing youth activities to continue much as before without the risk of a breach of the law.

Typical concerns that have been voiced are:

- where can our junior golfers go for a coffee or a soft drink after a round of golf?
- what about visiting youth teams – are their members accompanied if they are with their manager and/or coach?
- we have always staged our youth prizes presentation evenings in our main bar; will this have to change?

In addressing these questions it is important to remember that the statute prohibits unaccompanied children from being in "relevant premises" only when they are open for use for the supply of alcohol for consumption there. Premises are "relevant" for these purposes only if they are exclusively or primarily used for the supply of alcohol for consumption on the premises, or open for the supply of alcohol when a temporary event notice (see Chapter 9) is in place.

Thus, young golfers can have a drink or other refreshment in any part of the premises that is not relevant premises, or anywhere in the club premises at times when they are not open for the supply of alcohol. They can be given refreshments in an area set aside for changing, in the professional's shop, or in a pavilion or marquee, as long as those places are not part of the relevant premises. In addition, they are allowed to take refreshment in bars etc during times when they are not open for the supply of alcohol.

Turning to the question of visiting teams, whether or not a child is accompanied by a person who has attained the age of eighteen would be a matter to be determined by the court dealing with any prosecution under the section. It would a matter of fact to be decided on the evidence adduced. An important influencing factor might be the extent to which the accompanying adult can be said to be supervising the behaviour and activities of any particular child.

If, for example, fifteen under-age visiting rugby players and three reserves are found in a club bar during opening hours, in the company of one adult manager or coach, it might be stretching credulity to suggest that each one of the fifteen was accompanied in the way demanded by the legislation. On the other hand, should two young golfers come into a club bar during opening hours in the company of the club professional or the club captain, a court might be persuaded that they were properly accompanied.

Finally, clubs might need to review their practices on

presentation ceremonies. The hour set for the ceremony might be altered to make it possible for it to take place in the main bar. Alternatively, part of the club's premises that does not fall within the definition of "relevant premises" might be used for the function. In an extreme case, a club might have to arrange for the awards to be given at a different venue, such as a meeting room in the local town hall.

7. Unauthorised Licensable Activities

Section 136 of the Licensing Act 2003 deals with unauthorised licensable activities. In premises that are operated on the authority of a club premises certificate, only those licensable activities that are authorised in the certificate may lawfully be carried on there. If any unauthorised licensable activity is carried on there, or any attempt is made to carry it on, any person involved in the operation is guilty of the offence, if the person carried out, or attempted to carry out, the activity knowingly. For example, if regulated entertainment is provided in club premises when it is not one of the licensable activities referred to in the club's operating schedule, and therefore not authorised by the licensing authority, an offence would be committed.

Clearly, Parliament has decided that such offending is to be treated seriously since it has provided for a maximum fine of £20,000 – four times higher than the usual maximum for a single offence dealt with in the magistrates' courts. Alternatively, a term of imprisonment of up to six months may be imposed, or both a fine and a term of imprisonment may be ordered.

Where the activity in question is the provision of a "regulated entertainment", a person does not, however, commit an offence if his only involvement is that he:
- performs in a play;
- participates as a sportsman in an indoor sporting event;
- boxes or wrestles in a boxing or wrestling entertainment;
- performs live music;
- plays recorded music;
- performs dance; or
- performs certain entertainment similar to music or dance.

There is a statutory defence of "due diligence"; see below.

8. Exposing Alcohol for Unauthorised Sale (or Supply)

Section 137 of the Licensing Act provides that if alcohol is exposed for sale by retail in circumstances in which such sale would be an unauthorised licensable activity, the person exposing it in that way is guilty of an offence. "Exposing" for sale means exhibiting or displaying for sale. On conviction, such a person can be fined a sum not exceeding £20,000, imprisoned for up to six months, or both. In the case of members' clubs, the supply of alcohol is authorised only if a club premises certificate, that includes the sale or supply of alcohol as an authorised qualifying activity, is in force in relation to the relevant premises.

The alcohol in question, and the containers in which it is kept, may be forfeited by a court that convicts a defendant of this offence.

For the statutory defence of "due diligence"; see below.

9. Keeping Alcohol on Club Premises for Unauthorised Sale

A club's duty not to become involved in unauthorised supply begins when alcohol is brought into the premises. It is an offence for any officer or member of the club to be in possession of, or to have control of, alcohol that the officer or member intends to supply on behalf of the club, or to the order of a member of the club, in circumstances that are not authorised by the club's premises certificate.

A person convicted of an offence under these provisions is liable to a fine not exceeding £500. See section 138 of the Act.

There is a statutory defence of "due diligence"; see below.

10. Statutory Defence of Due Diligence

Section 139 of the Licensing Act 2003 sets out a defence which may be available to a person charged with carrying on an unauthorised licensable activity, exposing alcohol for unauthorised sale and keeping alcohol on premises for unauthorised sale (7, 8 and 9 above). In such cases it is open to the defendant to argue that the act was due to:
- a mistake;
- reliance on information given by someone else;
- an act or omission by another person; or
- some other cause beyond the defendant's control.

In addition, for the defence to succeed, it must be shown that the defendant took all reasonable precautions and exercised all due diligence to avoid committing the offence. The court would decide, as a matter of fact, whether the defendant had taken all the precautions that could have been taken, and exercised as much care as was practicable.

11. Allowing Disorderly Conduct on the Premises

Every officer or member of a club, and any person employed in club premises, whether paid or unpaid, is under a duty to ensure that the premises are conducted in an orderly fashion. Consequently, should any such person knowingly allow disorderly conduct to occur, that person is guilty of an offence and liable to a fine not exceeding £1,000 (section 140, Licensing Act 2003). This offence can be committed by any member or officer who was in the premises at the relevant time in a capacity which enabled the member or officer to prevent the disorderly conduct.

It is important to remember that, where such a charge is brought, it is for the prosecutor to prove, beyond reasonable doubt, that the defendant knew that the disorderly conduct was taking place. The offence is not an "absolute" offence.

12. Supply of Alcohol to a Person who is Drunk

Section 141 of the Licensing Act prohibits the supply of alcohol to a person who has already had enough to make him drunk. It is an offence for any member or officer of a club, or any person who works in a club, whether paid or unpaid, knowingly to supply or attempt to supply alcohol to a person who is drunk. It is also an offence for a person who is present on the premises in a capacity which enables that person to prevent it, knowingly to allow alcohol to be supplied to a drunken person. Once again, the fine that can be imposed for such an offence is up to £1,000.

It is also an offence for any person knowingly to obtain alcohol for consumption on the club's premises by a person who is drunk; the same maximum fine applies (section 142).

In the case of these offences the knowledge that the defendant must have had, if he is to be convicted, appears to be knowledge of the relevant person's state of sobriety. Since the view taken by a defendant must, of necessity, be a subjective view, the court must decide on the facts whether the view taken by the defendant was genuine and reasonably arrived at. It will be for the court to find, as a matter of fact, whether the opinion reached by the defendant, as to the relevant person's condition, was reasonable and genuine. The facts may lead the court to conclude that it could not have been. It is submitted, however, that the court should not convict on the basis that it would have come to a different subjective judgement of the person's state of sobriety.

13. Inspections

When an application for a club premises certificate is made, or an application for the variation or review of such a certificate is made, a constable authorised by the chief officer of police, and other authorised persons, are entitled to enter and inspect the premises to which the certificate relates. Section 96 of the Licensing Act 2003 contains the relevant provisions.

Any such entry and inspection must take place at a reasonable time, on a day not more than fourteen days after the making of the application. The Act stipulates that a person wishing to inspect premises under these powers must give at least forty-eight hours' notice of the intended visit to the club; the notice must specify the time and date at which it is intended to carry out the inspection.

The licensing authority may extend the time limit for making such an inspection, on the application of a responsible authority, but by not more than seven days. An extension of time may be granted only if it appears to the licensing authority that reasonable steps for an inspection to be made in good time were made, but that it was not possible for it to take place within the time allowed.

Any person who obstructs an authorised person or a constable in their exercise of these powers of entry and inspection is guilty of an offence. The maximum penalty is a fine not exceeding £500.

14. Other Powers of Entry and Search

In addition to the powers of entry and inspection mentioned above, section 97 gives police constables a general right to enter and search club premises in certain circumstances. This right may be exercised only if the officer has reasonable cause to believe that:

- an offence under section 4(3)(a), (b) or (c) of the Misuse of Drugs Act 1971 has been, is being, or is about to be, committed there. These are offences of supplying or offering to supply, or being concerned in supplying or making an offer to supply, a controlled drug; or
- there is likely to be a breach of the peace there.

In these circumstances the officer may, if necessary, use reasonable force to gain entry.

15. Training

The subject of staff, including training, is discussed in Chapter 16. In addition, all concerned in the management and running of a club need to have a full understanding of the statutory restrictions described in this chapter, and of the consequences of failure to comply.

Chapter 8

Club Rules

1. Introduction

Schedule 7 to the Licensing Act 1964 made specific provisions regarding matters that had to be dealt with in the rules of a registered club. They related to the general management of the club, the conduct of general meetings of members, membership and elective committees. The Licensing Act 2003 does not contain such a schedule. Rather, there is an expectation that the rules of the club are the yardstick by which licensing committees should judge whether a club qualifies for a premises certificate. Qualification is dealt with in Chapter 2. The rules of a club that is seeking a club premises certificate are, therefore, important. As noted in Chapter 4, when applying for a club premises certificate, the club must submit a copy of its rules. This enables the licensing authority to satisfy itself that the club is a qualifying club and that the club's operating schedule is not inconsistent with its rules.

Section 62 of the Licensing Act sets out the general conditions which a club must satisfy if it is to qualify for a club premises certificate. Some of those conditions relate to matters which the club must provide for in its rules:

- the admission of persons to membership of the club; and
- the establishment and conduct of the club in good faith as a members' club.

2. Rules Relating to Qualification

If a club is to qualify for a premises certificate, its rules must make provisions in relation to applications for, and admission to, membership. The rules must provide that a person may not be admitted to membership, or to the privileges of membership, without an interval of at least two days between the date the person is nominated, or applies, for membership, and the date of admission to membership. In addition, the rules must make clear that where a person becomes a member without application or nomination, that person may not be admitted to the privileges of membership until at least two days after becoming a member.

The rules should also make clear that when alcohol is supplied in the club's premises, such supply must be by or on behalf of the club. These requirements are dealt with in more detail in Chapter 2.

3.   Good Faith

Section 63 of the Licensing Act concerns the licensing authority's decision on whether or not a club is conducted "in good faith", that is, whether or not it is a genuine members' club – one that is run by the members for the benefit of the members, rather than one run for the benefit of an individual proprietor or proprietors. When making its decision, the licensing committee may consider, among other matters, the club's rules and arrangements concerning money, or other property of the club, or any gain that arises from carrying on the club. In particular, the licensing committee may take into account whether any such money, property or gain may be applied otherwise than for the benefit of the club as a whole, or for charitable, benevolent or political purposes. See also Chapter 2, pages 10–11.

The arrangements for giving members information about the finances of the club may also be taken into account. This is to enable the authority to satisfy itself that the members of the club retain control over the way in which it is managed and financed, and that they have access to the club's accounts.

The rules may also provide a useful vehicle for establishing that the additional conditions of qualification (those relating to the supply of alcohol) are also satisfied by the applicant club. Those conditions are set out in Chapter 2; see page 10.

4.   Rules Relating to the Management of Club Business

In the best-ordered clubs disputes may arise, from time to time, in relation to the way in which the business of the club is managed. To minimise such occurrences, the rules of a club ought to make specific provisions in relation to such matters, specifying who is to have authority to take decisions in any given circumstance, and how the club is to be run. Once the rules of the club have been drawn up they should be faithfully adhered to. Disputes will be comparatively rare if it can be shown without doubt that actions taken are within the rules. Likewise, if the rules are clear, it should be obvious when something has been done in contravention of the rules.

Of greatest importance are the rules that control the conduct of club business, delegated authorities, voting rights and the discipline of members. There should be very clear rules as to what business is to be transacted by all the members in a general meeting, and what decisions may be delegated to elected committees or officers.

The manner in which general meetings of members and committee meeting are conducted tends to be a fruitful source of contention in members' clubs. When difficulties arise, it is usually because the rules of the club are not sufficiently clear or comprehensive. When the rules are being drawn up, some care should be taken to ensure that potential difficulties are anticipated and that rules are included to reduce the likelihood of their occurring, and to provide for resolving them when they do arise. All rules should be expressed in clear, simple and unequivocal language.

A template for club rules is set out in Appendix C. Clubs that are affiliated to a parent society or association, such as the Club and Institute Union, usually adopt the model rules drawn up by the parent organisation.

The conduct of club meetings is dealt with in greater detail in Chapter 10.

5. The Duty to give Notice of Rule Changes

Club rules are not set in stone and may be amended when circumstances change. Maybe the aims and objects of the club have changed, or there has been a change of heart as to who may be admitted to membership. A club that has always been a club for men may decide that it wishes to open its door to women members, or *vice versa*. In such a case, a resolution comprising the proposed rule change should be put before the members in general meeting and adopted by them (see Chapter 10).

Schedule 8 to the Licensing Act 1964 dealt specifically with voting rights in clubs primarily for men or for women. It provided that in such clubs a rule that restricted voting to men or women, as the case may be, was not unlawful. Even after the repeal of the 1964 Act, but there is nothing in the 2003 Act that renders clubs run primarily for men, or for women, ineligible for club premises certificates.

If local authority licensing authorities are to operate in an efficient and effective way it is important that their records are up to date. Consequently, section 82 of the Licensing Act imposes a duty on a club which holds a club premises certificate to give the licensing authority prompt notice of any changes to its rules. The licensing authority is then under a duty to amend its records accordingly.

The onus of complying with this statutory requirement is borne by the club secretary. When a club changes any of its rules, the secretary must give notice of the alteration(s) to the chief executive of the licensing authority within twenty-eight days of the change being agreed. The notification must be accompanied by the club's premises certificate and the fee payable, currently £10.50.

If it is not possible to send the premises certificate to the licensing authority with the notification of rule change, the secretary must, instead, attach of statement of the reason for the failure to produce it. The local authority should be able to supply a copy of the premises certificate if it has been lost, stolen or mislaid (see page 39). It may charge a fee, currently £10.50, for supplying a copy document.

It is an offence for a club secretary to fail to give the required notice within the prescribed time limit. The penalty is a fine not exceeding £500.

Section 82 also imposes a duty on the club secretary to give notice to the local licensing authority of any change to the name of the club. The same procedures and penalties apply. The premises to which the club premises certificate relates cannot, though, be changed simply by giving notice under this section. Instead, the procedure for varying the premises to which the certificate relates, set out in Chapter 6, must be followed.

6. The Status of Club Rules Generally

Club rules form the blueprint for the proper management of a members' club. As mentioned above, some rules are required by statute. Clubs that are affiliated to parent bodies or are registered as industrial, provident or friendly societies must also include any rules that are required under the legislation controlling registration (see Chapter 2, pages 11–13). The rules of a club which is a limited company must reflect the requirements of the Companies Acts and its own memorandum and articles. Otherwise, the members of a club are free to determine the rules by which they wish their club to be run.

Questions often arise concerning the effect of a club's rules on a member's relationship with the club, and on the relationships between members. When a person joins a club, that person agrees to comply with the club rules. There is, in effect, a contract between the member and the club, and the rules by which the club is operated are taken to be terms of the contract. The rules are, therefore, binding on the member. This is so even if the member has not read the rules. If the rules are available to be read and are supplied to members when they join the club, the law assumes that they form the basis of a contract. Using the language of the law of contract, the club makes an offer to the prospective member that, in return for the payment of an annual or other periodic subscription, that person will be allowed to enjoy the benefits of membership as long as he or she accepts and complies with the club rules. In return, the prospective member agrees to pay the subscription and to comply with the rules. The offer is accepted and a contract comes into being.

It is when a member fails to comply with the terms of the contract, either by failing to pay the required subscription or by breaking club rules, that membership may be suspended or the offender may be expelled from membership.

Breaches of contract of this type would not usually come to the attention of the courts because they can be dealt with satisfactorily under the terms of the contract. The club rules are usually quite specific in relation to the consequences of a breach of them. The courts might be persuaded to intervene, however, if there is an allegation that the action taken by a club has resulted in some specific and quantifiable loss to the member, such as the loss of money or property. A member who believes that he has been expelled without justification, or wrongfully denied a specific right of membership, might persuade a court to intervene, but probably only if any rights of appeal under the rules have been exhausted. The rules might allow for an appeal to a specially appointed committee or panel of members, or they might allow for disputes over breaches of rules to be referred to independent arbitrators or mediators.

Chapter 9

Temporary Events

1. Introduction

From time to time, a member's club may find that it wishes to stage an event that cannot conveniently be held in its usual premises. The club may wish to boost its finances by holding a summer barbecue or a New Year Ball, or it may arrange prize presentation evenings that will attract greater numbers than can be accommodated comfortably in the club's certified premises.

Under the provisions of the Licensing Act 1964 it was possible for a club to hold an event in different premises simply by giving notice to the chief of police that on the specified date it would be using its registration certificate at alternative premises. Part 5 of the Licensing Act 2003 make new provisions for temporary activities. In the case of a members' club, the procedures are a little more complicated than those under the Licensing Act 1964, but they still provide a useful way in which a club may be allowed to use other premises for large functions.

2. Temporary Event Notice

If a club wishes to use alternative premises for licensable activities during any period that does not exceed ninety-six hours, a notice may be given to the relevant licensing authority that a temporary event is to be held there. The relevant licensing authority is the licensing authority for the area in which the premises where the event is to be held are situated. Thus it may be a different authority from the one which granted the club premises certificate.

A temporary event notice should be given by an individual, so, in the case of a member's club, it is convenient for the secretary or the member who is organising the event to give the required notice. The person who gives the notice becomes the "premises user" for the purposes of the event. A person giving a temporary event notice must be over the age of eighteen.

The provisions in relation to temporary events apply only if the number of persons expected to attend at any one time during the event is less than 500. Where the licensable activities at the event will include the supply of alcohol, it must be a condition of the notice that such supplies are to be made by or under the authority of the premises user.

An individual may give up to five temporary event notices in any year. No more than twelve notices may be given in respect of the same premises within the same year. These limits are different for a holder of a "personal licence" under the Act; but a club member or officer would not normally hold such a licence.

There must always be a gap of at least twenty-four hours between the end of one event period and the commencement of the next.

Temporary event procedures are not appropriate where a club needs to find alternative premises for an extended period, for example, while the club premises are being refurbished. If a club needs to use alternative premises for a continuous period in excess of ninety-six hours, the club must make an application under section 84, for the variation of the club premises certificate (see Chapter 6). On completion of the works, a further application must be made to vary the certificate once more so that it relates to the original club premises.

Two copies of the temporary event notice must be served on the relevant licensing authority no later than ten working days before the day on which the event period begins. The notice must be in a prescribed form, although at the time of going to press (March 2005), the form has not been prescribed. It must be accompanied by the appropriate fee, currently £21.00.

3. Police Objection

The police may object to the event if they are of the opinion that allowing the premises to be used in accordance with the notice would undermine the crime prevention objective of the legislation. This is the only ground upon which police may object. Any notice of objection must be given to the licensing authority no later than forty-eight hours after the date on which the chief officer is given a copy of the event notice.

Where notice of objection is given, the licensing authority must hold a hearing to consider the objection. Having held the hearing, the authority may consider it necessary, in the interests of promoting the crime prevention objective, to give a counter notice. A counter notice must be given to the premises user at least twenty-four hours before the beginning of the specified event period. If it is given within this time limit, the effect is that the premises user is prohibited from staging the event.

In some circumstances the police may, before the hearing, discuss their concerns with the premises user with a view to agreeing modifications to the temporary event notice which would meet the concerns of the police while allowing the event to proceed. Such an agreement may be reached at any time before a hearing is held to consider the police objection. Where such modifications are agreed, the notice of objection is withdrawn and the hearing is not necessary.

4.   Checklist

- The applicant must be over eighteen years of age;
- the event period must not exceed ninety-six hours;
- if there is to be more than one event, at least twenty-four hours must elapse between the end of one and the commencement of another;
- notice must be given to the relevant licensing authority not less than ten working days before the beginning of the event period;
- the event notice must include a condition that the supply of alcohol is to be under the authority of the premises user; and
- the appropriate fee must be sent with the notice.

5.   Rights of Entry

Constables and authorised officers (of a licensing authority) may enter premises to which a temporary event notice applies for the purpose of assessing the likely effect of the notice on the promotion of the crime prevention objective. An authorised officer must produce evidence of authority to exercise the power if requested to do so.

It is an offence for any person intentionally to obstruct an authorised officer exercising this power. The maximum penalty is a fine not exceeding £500.

6. The Duty to Keep and Produce Temporary Event Notices

When premises are being used on the authority of a temporary event notice, the premises user is under a duty to make sure that a copy of that notice is prominently displayed at the premises, or that the notice is in his custody or in the custody of another person, nominated for this purpose, who is working at the premises. Where such a nomination has been made, a notice of that fact, and the position held by the person who has been so nominated, must be prominently displayed at the premises. Failure to comply with these requirements is an offence; the maximum penalty is a fine not exceeding £500.

If the temporary event notice is not displayed at the event premises (and no notice as to the designated custodian of the notice is posted on them), a constable or authorised officer may require the premises user to produce the temporary event notice for examination. Again, if asked to do so, an authorised officer must produce evidence of authority to exercise this power.

Failure, without reasonable excuse, to produce a temporary event notice in accordance with a requirement made in this way is an offence. The maximum penalty is a fine not exceeding £500.

7. Lost or Stolen Temporary Event Notice

In the best ordered of organisations things can go wrong. However carefully important papers are guarded, it is still possible for them to be mislaid or misappropriated. The legislation acknowledges that fact and makes provision for duplicate documents to be obtained. The procedure for obtaining a duplicate of a club premises certificate, or a summary of such a document, is dealt with in Chapter 5 (see page 39). Section 110 of the Licensing Act makes similar provision for obtaining duplicate temporary event notices. These provisions may be important because the documents in question have to be produced when applications are made, or on the request of a police constable or an authorised officer of the licensing authority.

The fee payable for a certified copy of a temporary event notice is currently £10.50. The licensing authority is under a duty to supply the certified copy requested if it is satisfied that the original has been lost, stolen, damaged or destroyed and, where it has been lost or stolen, that the loss or theft has been reported to the police.

A copy issued under these provisions must be a copy of the document in the form in which it existed immediately before it was lost, stolen, damaged or destroyed. This requirement underscores the importance of the authority's duty, under section 93, to keep its records up to date.

Chapter 10

Meetings

1. Introduction

The statutory provisions relating to the management of club business are considered in Chapter 2. In this chapter, some of the common day-to-day problems that arise when transacting club business are considered. Experience indicates that disputes often concern the correct way to proceed with resolutions, elections or other business that needs to be dealt with by the members in general meeting or by committees using delegated powers. Perhaps it is not surprising that difficulties arise, given that many of those responsible for managing the affairs of members' clubs are volunteers whose positions are honorary. Members' clubs cannot always afford to employ full-time professional officers experienced in the conduct of formal business meetings.

In this chapter the focus is on recognised best practices in relation to the conduct of business meetings, although some of the statutory controls are also mentioned.

Clubs affiliated to national organisations or to the Club and Institute Union may find that they are expected to follow specific procedures set out in a manual provided by the organisation. The guidance given in this chapter will be of greatest benefit to those clubs that have no such allegiance.

2. Old Clubs

Problems may arise in relation to the conduct of a general meeting of members as a result of an omission from the Licensing Act 2003. Whether by accident, oversight or design, certain statutory provisions that have been an important part of the legislation relating to

70

members' clubs have not been repeated in the new Act. Curiously, the omissions in question are likely to give rise to marked differences in the running of clubs that were registered under the Licensing Act 1964 and those which obtain new club premises certificates under the 2003 Act.

Schedule 7 to the 1964 Act made provisions in relation to club rules. That schedule imposed obligations on registered clubs in relation to:

- the management of the club;
- general meetings;
- membership; and
- elective committees.

In relation to general meetings, the schedule provides:

- that there must be a general meeting of the club at least once a year and that there must not be more than fifteen months between general meetings;
- that both the general committee and the members must be capable of summoning meetings;
- that general meetings must be confined to members;
- that all members entitled to use the club premises must be entitled to vote and have equal voting rights (no casting vote for the chairman); and
- for exceptions to the general rules in relation to voting rights in certain specified circumstances.

The exceptions concerning voting rights may be summarised as follows:

- there may be a rule that excludes from voting members under a certain age, women if the club is primarily for men, or men if the club is primarily for women;
- if the club is primarily for former members of Her Majesty's Forces, persons who have not been in the services may be excluded from voting;
- if club rules provide for family membership or family subscriptions, persons who use the club by virtue of being a member of a family but who are not themselves members may be excluded from voting.

The schedule also requires clubs to have at least one elective committee. An elective committee must consist of members of the club, elected each year at a general meeting for a period of not less than twelve months and not more than five years. Elections have to be held annually and, if all the elected members are not to go out of office each year, the rules must make clear which of them are to go out of office each year. The schedule allows for casual vacancies to be filled by appointment.

Elective committees are expected to deal with all matters that are not reserved for decision by the members in general meeting. It follows that the rules of a members' club should spell out which matters are to be decided by the members and which may be delegated to elective committees or to club officers.

The Act of 1964 does not contain any requirements as to the election of officers. It is left for the members to decide whether the officers of the club should be elected by the members in general meeting or whether, having elected a committee to manage the club's day-to-day affairs, it should be left to that committee to elect its own chairman and secretary. Typically, the members of a club elect a club chairman, club secretary and honorary treasurer, and those officers become *ex officio* members of the elective committee.

The statutory provisions referred to above have not been replicated in the Licensing Act 2003. Even so, a club registered under the 1964 Act continues to be bound by the provisions of Schedule 7 if it is granted a premises certificate under the transitional provisions described in Chapter 3. This is because, although the 1964 Act is repealed completely upon the coming into full force of the 2003 Act, the new certificate is granted subject to conditions which reproduce the effect of any restriction imposed on the use of the premises for the existing qualifying club activities. Regulations made pursuant to the Licensing Act 2003 make clear that the Licensing Act 1964 falls within this provision. As a consequence, existing members' clubs continue to be required to comply with the requirements in relation to general meetings set out in the 1964 Act.

3. New Clubs

Potential difficulties arise in relation to clubs that obtain premises certificates under the provisions of Part 4 of the Licensing Act 2003. Where no representations are made in relation to an application, the licensing authority may impose only such conditions as are consistent with the club operating schedule, and the mandatory conditions set out in sections 73 (concerning off-sales; see page 31) and 74 (concerning the showing of films on club premises; see page

32) of the Act. Even where representations have been made, the licensing authority is authorised to impose only such additional conditions as are necessary for the promotion of the licensing objectives.

Even if licensing authorities appreciate the potential difficulties resulting from the failure to provide statutory controls over the conduct of club meetings, it is unlikely that they will be able to assist by imposing conditions similar to those contained in Schedule 7 to the 1964 Act, described above, since it is difficult to see how such conditions could be said to be necessary for the promotion of the licensing objectives.

If a new club is free from the constraints of the 1964 Act, there is a risk that its affairs may fall into the hands of a minority who may seek to run it in a way that does not meet the wishes of the majority. The best safeguard would be for members to agree, voluntarily, to adopt rules that reflect the conditions set out in Schedule 7 to the 1964 Act, even though the Act will have been repealed by the time their club applies for a club premises certificate.

4. Challenges by Members

If difficulties do arise once a club premises certificate has been obtained, perhaps because of the absence of democratic management, there may be several courses open to aggrieved members. One possibility is that they may be able to convince the licensing authority that there are grounds for a review of the relevant premises certificate. Such a course of action would, however, succeed only if the authority is satisfied that the grounds for the application are relevant to one or more of the licensing objectives contained in section 4(2) – the prevention of crime and disorder; public safety; the prevention of public nuisance; or the protection of children from harm. Otherwise, the application for review would be rejected.

Another possibility is that a sufficient number of members may be prepared to support a vote of no confidence in the officers and/or the management committee. It is arguable, however, that the elected committee would not be bound to act upon such a resolution and arrange for new elections to be held unless the rules of the club specifically allowed for the removal of officers or committees on the basis of a motion of no confidence. The argument is that without such a provision in club rules, any decision that officers or committee members be removed from office would be *ultra vires*.

Another approach that dissatisfied members may be able to take is to question whether their club is being conducted in good faith. A members' club must be established and conducted in good faith if it is to be regarded as a qualifying club (see Chapter 2). This course of action would require members to contact the licensing authority to suggest that their club no longer qualifies for a club premises certificate since it is no longer established and conducted in good faith. If the licensing authority is satisfied that the allegation is true, it has the power to withdraw the premises certificate in accordance with section 90 of the Act. If necessary, the licensing authority may call upon the police, persuading them to apply to the magistrates for a warrant to enter the club premises and search them for evidence in support of the allegation that the club is no longer established and run in good faith. This procedure is described in Chapter 5 (see pages 41–42).

The disadvantage of this course of action would be that, if it is successful, the club's premises certificate would be withdrawn. A new application for a club premises certificate would have to be made if the members wish to continue to operate as a members' club, and it would then be for the members to convince the licensing authority that the club once more qualifies for a certificate in that it is again established and conducted in good faith.

5. Delegated Powers

Whatever the statutory position, the health and well-being of a members' club depends on its affairs being conducted in a regular and transparent fashion, and in the best interests of the members generally. Problems can arise when attempts are made to run a members' club otherwise than in accordance with recognised business procedures. Club rules can be used to prescribe the procedures to be followed. If so, each rule must be set out in simple, clear, unequivocal language to keep any disputes to a minimum.

When a decision needs to be made in relation to the running of a members' club, it is necessary to consider first whether the matter must be referred to the members as a whole, or whether the officers or a club committee can deal with the matter under delegated powers. Generally, proposals for changes to the constitution of a club, or to its principal objectives or rules, should be put before all the members for decision. Matters relating to the day-to-day running of the club, such as the employment of staff, the ordering of stock and services and the maintenance of order and discipline, are probably best dealt with by the committee or an officer. It is vital that the club rules specify which matters must be decided by all the members, and which are to be delegated.

The manner in which delegated powers are to be exercised may also need to be spelt out in the rules. For example, where an officer or committee has the authority to conduct proceedings in relation to allegations of indiscipline, the rules should specify how those proceedings should be conducted and what rights the member has at the disciplinary hearing. Difficulties may arise if these matters are not clearly defined in the rules.

If officers have the power to act on behalf of the members, they can make executive decisions that are binding on the members. If a club committee has power to take a decision, it is able to discuss the matter and reach a conclusion which, again, binds the members.

Delegated powers do not have to be exercised. If the matter to be resolved is particularly sensitive or might prove controversial, the officer or committee concerned may decide to refer it to a meeting of all the members for discussion and determination, even though the officer or committee has delegated authority.

Where there is no delegated authority to resolve a particular issue, or it has been decided that such authority is not to be invoked, a general meeting of members must be called. A resolution should be drawn up and publicised, and the members should be asked to vote on that resolution and any amendments that may be submitted.

6. General Meetings

Convening a General Meeting

Club rules should include provisions relating to the calling of general meetings and those rules should be adhered to. In the interests of minimising disagreement about procedures, clubs should take into account the statutory requirements set out at the beginning of this chapter. Every member who is entitled to attend a general meeting and to vote on issues raised for discussion should be given reasonable notice of the date and time of the meeting and the venue for it. The notice should give full details of the matters to be discussed and the decisions to be made. Any decision taken without proper notice being given to members is open to challenge by one of the methods described on pages 73–74 above. The club rules should make clear what is to be regarded as reasonable notice. It is suggested that, in the absence of emergency, a minimum of seven days' notice should be given.

Sometimes difficulties arise because attempts are made during general meetings to deal with matters that were not canvassed in the notice convening the meeting. The temptation to do so should be resisted. This is because a member who has chosen not to attend the meeting on the basis of the information given in the convening notice may, justifiably, complain that he would have attended and taken part had he known the other issue was to be determined.

It is strongly recommended that the general provisions contained in Schedule 7 to the 1964 Act be incorporated in club rules and adhered to. Such rules would then fix the frequency with which general meetings are to be held; establish the basis upon which extraordinary meetings may be called; and provide that at general meetings of the club, every member who is entitled to vote is allowed to do so and every member, including the person chairing the meeting, is to have an equal vote. The chairman should not have a casting vote at general meetings.

Voting

Recognised business practice requires that any proposition or resolution that is put before the members must have the support of more than fifty per cent of the voting members if it is to be adopted. If there is a tie, or if fewer than fifty per cent of the voting members give their support to the resolution, it should be declared to have been lost.

Amendments to any resolution that is put before the members should be allowed. Where an amendment is tabled, it should be voted upon first. If more than fifty per cent of the voting members support the amendment, it is agreed and the original resolution should be declared to have been lost. If the amendment fails to gain the required support, it should be declared to have been lost and the original resolution should then be put to the vote.

If several amendments have been tabled they should be voted upon in turn, until such time as one of them receives the support of more than fifty per cent of the voting members. At that point the successful amendment should be declared adopted and the original resolution should not be put to a vote. If all amendments fail to receive the required support, a vote should be taken on the original resolution.

Minutes should be taken of the matters raised and the decisions reached at the general meeting, and the club rules should provide for the proper dissemination of those minutes to members.

7. Committee Meetings

Terms of Reference

Licensing legislation has never contained provisions regulating the manner in which the general decision-making processes in members' clubs should be delegated, or the way in which officers or elected committees should reach their decisions or conduct their business. It has always been left to the members to decide issues of delegation, and the decisions reached by them in that regard should be enshrined in the club's rules.

The matters that should be delegated, and to whom, are often self-evident, the decisions being driven by practical considerations. For example, it would be wholly impracticable for all the members to have to make day-to-day decisions affecting the running of the club's affairs or to negotiate contracts with suppliers and others doing work for the benefit of members. The members as a whole could not be actively concerned in the recruitment and interviewing of staff, although the number of staff to be employed and the level of wages to be paid may be matters to be agreed in general meeting. Again, when disciplinary action against an individual member needs to be taken it would not, as a general rule, be practicable for the members to be involved, even though decisions about the sort of behaviour that might lead to disciplinary action might be agreed by the members generally.

It is important that club rules deal, in unambiguous terms, with who is authorised to deal with what, and the basis upon which delegated powers are to be exercised. For the avoidance of doubt, the rules may also be used as a vehicle for ensuring that club committees are run on proper, business-like lines and that all those entitled to participate in decisions are able to do so.

Convening Committee Meetings

Elected members of any committee should be given proper notice of the dates and times of meetings. Generally, the business at such meetings should follow a published agenda, although it might be agreed in urgent cases that a matter be discussed and determined even though it was not mentioned in the agenda. It is not usually necessary for the committee secretary to send each committee member formal notice of each meeting. Meetings may be scheduled on a fixed basis, for example, on the third Wednesday in each month, or the dates of meetings might be fixed in advance for a period of, say, twelve months. Each committee member would then be responsible for being present at committee meetings, and the secretary would give notice only of any changes to the published arrangements.

The Conduct of Meetings

The rules should specify a quorum for any committee meeting, and that business should not be transacted if the required number of members is not present at the meeting. In the latter circumstances, the meeting should be postponed until the minimum number of members is able to attend. Business transacted in the absence of the necessary quorum is void.

A person should be elected to chair committee meetings, and a person should be nominated or elected to take a note of the matters raised and the decisions taken. All members should be entitled to see the minutes taken at committee meetings, so it is important that the matters discussed and the decisions taken are properly recorded.

Difficulties often arise in relation to the keeping and publishing of committee minutes. It is often argued that if minutes have to be made available to all the members, free and frank discussion of agenda items may be inhibited. Matters relating to the conduct or discipline of members tend to give rise to the greatest degree of concern. Committee members frequently argue that they could not be completely open about their views if their comments must then be made available to any member who may wish to see them. This difficulty usually arises because of a misunderstanding about the nature of minutes. Minutes need be only a brief summary of the proceedings at a meeting. They should not take the form of a verbatim account of the discussions. They should set out each of the items raised for discussion and/or decision and record the decisions reached as a result. Minutes should not contain the detail of the discussions that gave rise to the decisions reached. If the correct style is used for minutes and the detailed discussions are regarded as confidential to committee members, the members can be kept in touch with the decisions being made on their behalf while minimising the risk of bad feeling.

The statutory requirements in relation to voting that apply in the case of general meetings of the club (see above) do not apply to committee meetings. Specifically, while good practice demands that every member of a committee should have a vote whenever a decision is to be made, the person chairing the meeting can be given a casting vote in the interests of ensuring that progress is made in all discussions and to avoid stalemate situations. If the rules for committee meetings allow it, the person in the chair can resolve any stalemate by recording a casting vote.

A question which sometimes arises is whether a member of a committee may abstain from voting on a particular proposition. The answer is that committee members are not compelled to cast a vote, any more than it is possible to force any enfranchised adult to vote in a general or local election. If, though, a committee member were to make a practice of abstaining, the broader issue of whether that person should remain a member of the committee may arise. If a member rarely contributes to the decision-making process that person's worth as a member of the committee may well be open to question.

When the result of a ballot is being determined, abstentions should be recorded and taken into account. In some cases an abstention may have the effect of a vote against the motion, since it may result in a failure to achieve a majority in support. Without majority support any motion is of course lost.

Maintaining Numbers of Members
Ordinarily, the composition of a club committee should be determined by the members of the club and set out in the club's rules. The persons to serve on it are elected at the annual general meeting. The rules should specify the period during which each elected committee member should hold office. Typically, the rules provide for a system of retirement by rotation, with retiring members being eligible for re-election should they wish to be considered for a further period in office. It is quite common to find that, initially, some members are elected for three years, some for two years and some for one year. The number of votes cast determines who is elected for

which period of time, those with the highest number being elected for the longest period and those with the smallest vote serving for the shortest term.

The numbers serving on a committee may be reduced: a member may find that other commitments make it impossible to continue to serve; a member may move away from the area; or there may be a death or incapacity that gives rise to a depletion of committee numbers. It is prudent for clubs to anticipate such eventualities and to make provision in the rules for filling casual vacancies. Some clubs may prefer to call an extraordinary general meeting and hold an election to find a replacement member. Others may be content to give the committee authority to co-opt a member onto the committee to fill the vacancy until the next scheduled elections are held.

The Election of Officers

In some clubs, the officers elected by the members in general meeting automatically serve on the club's management committee. On the other hand, the affairs of a club may be entrusted to a number of committees rather than a single management committee. For example, a club may have a "bar committee" which oversees the supply of alcohol to members and guests, and an "entertainments committee" which takes responsibility for engaging entertainers and organising functions. In such cases there are no statutory controls in relation to the election of officers. Ordinarily, it is for the members of each committee to elect one of their colleagues to take the chair at meetings and another to act as secretary. The rules should make clear whether committees have the delegated authority to take such decisions.

Chapter 11

Officers and Trustees

1. Introduction

The officers and, where appropriate, trustees, of a members' club play an important part in the management and conduct of the club. The role played by particular officers may vary somewhat from club to club. In some clubs, all the officers may hold office in an honorary capacity. In others, the club's activities may be such that certain officers are paid to carry out their duties. Some of the officers, whether paid or unpaid, are liable in law for any breaches of statutory requirements that may occur at the club. A grasp of the general duties of the officers and trustees is essential if members' clubs are to be managed effectively and in accordance with the law.

2. The Chairman

The chairman of a members' club has an important role. The chairman usually chairs general meetings of the members and, along with the other officers of the club, is responsible for seeing that the club is run smoothly and in accordance with the rules. It follows that the chairman must be fully familiar with all aspects of the club's rules and aims and objectives. The chairman should also be fully aware of any obligations, legal or otherwise, that the club may have.

Along with the club secretary, it is the chairman who is liable to prosecution if the licensing laws are broken by the club, but the chairman is not usually personally liable for the club's debts unless the chairman has entered into a contract on behalf of the club that was not authorised by the club. The chairman is often the public face of the club and so should behave in a manner that is above reproach at all times.

Arguably, the most important responsibility the chairman has is in relation to general meetings of members. It is the chairman who is responsible for the proper conduct of the meeting, and so should have confidence and an air of authority that will ensure that discussions take place in an orderly, sensible fashion and in accordance with the rules of the club and the provisions of licensing legislation.

3. The Secretary

The club secretary is responsible for ensuring that the instructions of the committee in relation to the every-day running of the club are carried out. The secretary should ensure that important club documents and authorisations are kept safely, and maintain proper club records, of, for example, members' names and addresses.

The secretary has certain duties under the Licensing Act 2003. The secretary must ensure that the licensing authority is notified of any change of name and of any alteration to the club rules. The secretary should also take responsibility for giving notice of any change of relevant registered address for the club. Most importantly, the club secretary is responsible for ensuring that the club's premises certificate is kept under the control of a nominated person and that a summary of it is prominently displayed on the club's premises, along with a notice specifying the position held by the nominated person. The secretary commits an offence if this statutory provision is not met.

4. The Treasurer

The Licensing Act 1964 contained a provision that a club should be considered to be conducted in good faith only if it had satisfactory arrangements for giving members proper information about the finances of the club, and allowed them access to the books of account and other records kept, to enable them to ensure the accuracy of that information.

These provisions have been replicated and expanded in the 2003 Act. Section 63 states that, in considering whether a club is established and conducted in good faith as a members' club, account is to be taken, among other matters, of:
- any provision in the rules or arrangements under which money or property of the club, or any gain from carrying on the club,

is or may be applied otherwise than for the benefit of the club as a whole or for charitable, benevolent or political purposes;
- the arrangements for giving members information about the finances of the club, and
- the books of account and other records kept to ensure the accuracy of that information.

Generally, it is the members of a club who elect a treasurer and appoint an auditor or auditors to oversee the accounts. These elections and appointments should be made at the annual general meeting and notice of them should be given as items for determination by the members. In many clubs the position of club treasurer may be purely honorary, but in large clubs a salary or stipend may be paid.

The office of treasurer is not one that should be taken on without mature consideration. Some statutory duties do have to be shouldered by the treasurer. For example, the treasurer is responsible for ensuring that the club complies with tax laws. The duties may include dealing with salaries, income tax and capital gains tax as well as the payment of invoices and accounts tendered to the club for payment. The treasurer may also be responsible for levying membership fees and keeping proper accounts in relation to them. The treasurer is also responsible for the conduct of the club's banking business.

The treasurer does not, however, carry out these duties independently. The management committee gives directions with regard to financial transactions, the treasurer making such payments as are directed and generally dealing with funds in accordance with the wishes of the committee. In certain circumstances, financial matters may be referred to the members in general meeting. The treasurer is bound to act on any decisions the members take in respect of those matters.

Generally, the treasurer has no personal liability for the debts of the club, but may become liable for acts outside the instructions given, or by acting in excess of delegated authority. For example, if the treasurer were to enter into a contract for the supply of goods that was not authorised by the members or the management committee, the treasurer could be held personally liable for the debt to the supplier.

5.   Trustees

A members' club does not have to have trustees to be a qualifying club for the purposes of the Licensing Act 2003. But trustees may be appointed if there is a need for club property or assets to be held in trust by a group of trustees who will take care of the property or assets on behalf of the members. Many clubs are unincorporated associations and so are unable to hold property in the name of the club. Named individuals must hold the property on behalf of the club, and they must hold it in trust for the benefit of all the members. Members' clubs that are incorporated, such as those that are limited companies or associations registered as provident or industrial societies, are able to hold property in their corporate names, and so do not need trustees to hold property on the members' behalf.

In general terms, the duty of trustees is to hold property in trust for the members of the club. Trustees are not usually expected to play any part in the management of the club, although they are bound to carry out any instructions they are given in relation to the club's property by the management committee. They do, however, have a duty to make sure that the property is preserved and its value is maintained by ensuring that assets are used properly and not put at risk by improper or reckless action taken by those who manage the club's affairs.

The precise nature of the trustees' responsibilities may be determined by reference to a number of sources. First, there is the deed of trust drawn up when the trust was set up. That document should contain details of the trustees' duties, powers and responsibilities in relation to the trust property. The trustees are bound by that deed and expected to comply with it at all times.

Next, the general law of trusts is of relevance. This body of law is wide and complex. Even so, the trustees must comply with it, and are liable to a civil action for breach of trust if they contravene it.

The rules of the club may also be relevant. In many instances the rules make specific provision for the appointment of trustees; their term of office; how they may be replaced; and the rights they have, if any, to attend meetings and to vote on resolutions put before the members. If they are members as well as trustees, they are enfranchised. They may also be given the right to attend committee meetings, although they are not likely to be able to vote on matters being decided by the committee since they have not been elected as members of it.

Finally, in the case of clubs affiliated to a parent organisation, such as the Royal British Legion or a political association, the trustees may be expected to comply with national guidelines. The adoption of model rules in relation to trustees has obvious advantages. The club can be reasonably sure that the national guidelines have been fully considered and deal with all the important issues in relation to trustees. In addition, by adopting a national model, the management committee is relieved of the onerous task of drafting rules that adequately cover all aspects of the subject.

As a general rule, trustees do not have any personal liability in relation to the debts incurred by the club. Nor are they liable for any compensation or damages that may be ordered in respect of actions brought against the club. Trustees should be aware, however, that should it be found that the members of the club have suffered a financial loss as a result of negligence on their part or failure by them to carry out their duties as trustees, they could be sued for breach of trust and ordered to compensate the members.

Chapter 12

Staff

1. Introduction

While in some members' clubs the work to keep the operation running is done by members, in most clubs it is undertaken by employees. Many members' clubs are employers and so need to be aware of the law relating to employment. The officers and committee members are responsible for ensuring that the club complies with the law. Statutory provisions affect all stages of employment, from recruitment and appointment of staff, to conditions of employment, and on to termination of contracts. Discipline and the maintenance of order have to be dealt with in any club and those who are responsible for those matters need to be aware of the statutory constraints.

The law relating to employment is wide and complex and it is beyond the scope of this manual to deal with it comprehensively, but in this chapter, some of the more important points are highlighted.

2. Recruitment and Appointment

Direct Discrimination

When employing staff, care must be taken to avoid discrimination. The Sex Discrimination Act 1975, the Race Relations Act 1976 and the Disability Discrimination Act 1995 all have an impact on the way in which jobs are advertised and appointments are made.

Under the terms of these Acts, discrimination on grounds of sex, race or disability is prohibited. The most obvious form of discrimination is direct discrimination, that is, when a person is treated less favourably than another person would be treated because of sex, marital status or race, or because of a disability. Under the Sex Discrimination and Race Discrimination Acts, the prohibition applies to both direct and indirect discrimination. Under the Disability Discrimination Act it applies only to direct discrimination, and clubs having fewer than twenty employees are exempt from the provisions that relate to employment. The rest of the Act, however, notably the sections concerning the provision of goods and services, applies to all clubs.

In determining whether there has been discrimination, a tribunal would consider whether the claimant was treated less favourably than another person and whether that treatment was due, in some causative sense, to the claimant's sex, race or disability.

For example, if a club were to advertise for a *barman,* a female applicant may have a claim for sex discrimination if she could show that she was treated differently from other applicants for the job and that her treatment was due to the fact that she is a woman. Her claim would be unlikely to succeed, however, if the employer could show that, despite the wording of the advertisement, all applicants were treated in the same way and that the fact that she was not appointed was for reasons unrelated to her sex, for example, the greater experience of the person appointed.

It is for the industrial tribunal to decide whether a claimant has been treated less favourably than others; the claimant's own subjective belief is not sufficient to establish that there has been discrimination: see the case of *Burrett v West Birmingham Health Authority.*

For a claim to succeed, it must be shown that a difference in treatment was on the ground of sex, race or disability and not for some other, valid reason. If applicants are treated in different ways because of the employer's practical experience rather than because of their sex, race or physical ability, there is no discrimination. In the case of *Noble v David Gold and Son (Holdings) Ltd*, the employer allocated female staff to lighter work than male employees because his experience showed that the women would not be able to do the heavier work. This was held not to be discrimination.

The work carried out in club premises is generally capable of being undertaken efficiently by men or women, and regardless of race. Care should be taken to avoid wording advertisements so as to suggest that only men or only women will be considered, or that persons of certain races should not apply. Clearly, an advertisement for a white, male cleaner under the age of fifty, or for female bar staff between the ages of twenty and thirty-five would be likely to put the club in a difficult situation should a claim for discrimination be made.

Indirect Discrimination

The concept of indirect discrimination is, perhaps, a little more difficult to understand. Under the Sex Discrimination Act and the Race Relations Act, indirect discrimination occurs when an employer applies a requirement or condition which, even though it applies equally to all persons:

- is such that the proportion of people of one sex or race who can comply with it is considerably smaller than the proportion in another;
- the employer cannot show that it is justifiable otherwise than on grounds of sex or race; and
- is detrimental to the complainant because the complainant cannot comply with it.

A requirement or condition means something that has to be complied with. Where there are no requirements or conditions relating to an appointment, an employer is entitled to take into account factors such as the applicant's practical experience in England, and ability to communicate in English. In the case of *Perera v Civil Service Commission and Department of Customs and Excise (No. 2)*, it was held that the only condition of appointment was that the applicant should be a barrister or solicitor. Since the complainant was so qualified, that condition was of no detriment to him. Factors that are plus or minus points that could apply to all applicants may be taken into account. They do not amount to discrimination against any particular applicant.

Examples of factors which have been held to be requirements or conditions include refusal to employ a person with young children since this would affect considerably more married than unmarried persons (*Thorndyke v Bell Fruit (North Central) Ltd*); and refusal to hire persons resident in a particular postal district where fifty per cent of the population were black (*Hussein v Saints Complete House Furnishers Ltd*).

Just as discrimination, or any suggestion of it, is to be avoided when posts are advertised, so the interviewing and appointment procedures must not be such as to treat some applicants less favourably than others. A female interviewee should not be asked if she plans to have children, or about how her children might affect her ability to do the job. Such questions are unlikely to be asked of a male applicant and it could be alleged that the female applicant is being treated less favourably than her male counterpart.

The Equal Opportunities Commission recommends that job age limits should be retained only if they are necessary to the job (for example, where a licence is required to do the job and such a licence is not available until a certain age); that job applications from men and women should be processed in exactly the same way; and that questions about marriage plans and family intentions should not be asked, as they could be construed as showing a bias against women. Clubs should keep these guidelines in mind when dealing with recruitment, interviews and appointments.

The Equal Opportunities Commission provides advice to both employers and employees. It is based at Arndale House, Arndale Centre, Manchester M4 3EQ; telephone (0845) 601 5901. Its website address is www.eoc.org.uk.

3.   **Contracts of Employment and Job Descriptions**

A contract of employment, like any other contract, comes into being when the terms of an offer of employment made by one party, the employer, are accepted by the other party, the employee. The popular concept that to be binding a contract must be in writing is a myth. The conditions of a contract of employment, however, may be evidenced by a number of different sources, including a contract document if there is one; terms incorporated from documents such as letters between the parties; and job descriptions. In addition, certain terms may be implied, while some may be imposed by statute.

Employers are under a duty to provide employees with a written statement of certain terms of their employment. Such statements must be provided within two months of the commencement of employment. A wise employer not only supplies this statement of limited terms but also enters into a contract that contains, in addition to the obligatory terms, all the other terms and conditions of the agreement that will govern the future working relationship between the parties.

It may be that circumstances change and that the club would like to alter the terms of employment or job description of a member of staff. Once made, though, it may not be easy to change the terms of a contract. The general rule is that the terms of a contract, including the job description where appropriate, can be changed only with the agreement of both parties. Careful thought should be given to the wording of a job description in the first place, especially if some flexibility may be needed as the club develops. Provided it is not unreasonable, a "catch-all" condition of employment may prove invaluable. A concluding sentence in the job description to the effect that, in addition to the specified tasks, the employee will be expected to carry out any other tasks that the employer may reasonably ask the employee to undertake is not uncommon. Of course, the request will not be reasonable if the work to be undertaken is specialist work beyond the competence of the employee in question.

4. Termination of Employment

By Notice

Unless a contract is for a fixed term, in which case it comes to an end on the expiry of the specified period, employment is taken to be for an indefinite period but subject to termination by the giving of reasonable notice. Often the period of notice to be given, by either the employer or the employee, is one of the matters agreed between the parties at the beginning of the employment. Where there is such an agreement, the period should be set out in the written particulars of employment.

In the absence of an agreed period of notice, the law is that a "reasonable" period of notice must be given. What is reasonable in any particular case depends on the employment in question. In many instances, the payment interval is taken to be a reasonable period. For example, weekly wage earners are usually required to give and entitled to receive one week's notice, while in the case of a person employed on a monthly salary, one month's notice is usually deemed reasonable. The importance of the particular job to the employer's organisation may demand a longer period in which to find a replacement, but in such a case it is to be expected that the period would be agreed in advance and set out in the terms of employment.

The Employment Rights Act 1996 provides for a minimum period of notice. An employer must give an employee a minimum of one week's notice if the employee has been employed for between one month and two years; and an additional week's notice for each year of employment thereafter, up to a maximum of twelve weeks where employment has lasted for twelve years or more. An employee who has been in employment for more than one month must give a minimum of one week's notice.

The statute does not prevent the parties from agreeing to waive the statutory period of notice, or from agreeing a payment in lieu of notice. Nor does the statute affect the right of an employer to terminate a contract without the statutory notice where the employee has been guilty of misconduct.

Whether an employer is entitled to make a payment in lieu of notice if the employee wishes to work out his notice is uncertain: see the case of *Marshall (Cambridge) Ltd v Hamblin*. It is clear that where the right to notice is waived, the right to payment in lieu of notice is lost: *Trotter v Forth Ports Authority* and *Baldwin v British Coal Corporation*.

During periods of notice the rate of payment made to the employee must be the usual weekly or monthly rate. This is so even if the employee does not work during the period.

Following a Breach of Contract
A contract of employment may come to an end if there is a fundamental breach of the contract terms. Such breaches may consist of a breach of a term or condition which:

- is considered by the parties to be vital: see the case of *The Mihalis Angelos*;
- has such serious consequences that the other party to the contract is deprived of that which he contracted for: *Hong Kong Fir Shipping v Kawasaki Kisen Kaisha*;
- demonstrates that the other party does not intend to continue to be bound by one or more of the terms or conditions: *Western Excavating (EEC) Ltd v Sharpe*.

A series of smaller breaches may constitute a fundamental breach. The last of a number of comparatively minor breaches of contract may be enough to cause the other party to consider the contract at an end: *Garner v Grange Furnishing Ltd*.

By Dismissal
The law recognises that, as a general rule, a dismissal is lawful providing the proper notice is given. There are exceptional circumstances which may affect this, but they are unlikely to arise in relation to members' clubs.

In certain circumstances an employee's contract may be

terminated without notice, that is, he may be summarily dismissed. For summary dismissal to be justified, it is necessary to show that the conduct complained of is such that the employee has been shown to disregard the essential conditions of his contract of employment: *Laws v London Chronicle (Indicator Newspapers) Ltd.* Examples of gross misconduct are theft from the employer, or other act of dishonesty against the employer, and gross insubordination.

There may be a case of "constructive dismissal" if an employee resigns because conduct on the part of the employer gives rise, in the opinion of the employee, to a fundamental breakdown in the trust that should exist between employer and staff. Where constructive dismissal is found to have occurred, the employee is entitled to compensation and/or damages, even though he was the person who brought the contract of employment to an end.

5.   Working Time

The United Kingdom government has adopted European directives controlling working time and the employment of young workers. The terms of these directives have been incorporated in the Working Time Regulations 1998 (Statutory Instrument 1998 No. 1833). These regulations apply to workers and employees. There are certain exceptions and exemptions in the regulations, but none that would be relevant to members' clubs.

The general purpose of the regulations is that any person who works for another, whether or not on the basis of a contract of employment, should have the protection of the European directives. The position of persons who work on a casual or agency basis is not entirely clear, usually because it is uncertain whether there is an employer against whom any proceedings may properly be taken. Any application to a tribunal or county court to enforce the regulations would be determined on the basis of the facts of the particular case.

Limit on Hours

The object of the Working Time Regulations is to safeguard the health and safety of workers. The principal safeguard is a limit on the number of hours that an employee may be asked to work in any week. In the case of an adult worker, the maximum number of hours that may be worked in any week is forty-eight. However, the limit applies to the average number of hours worked over a seventeen-week reference period. A worker may lawfully be asked to work for more than forty-eight hours in a particular week as long as the average over the reference period does not exceed forty-eight hours. By way of example, if a worker puts in forty hours a week for twelve weeks, then works ten hours' overtime for the next five weeks, the average working time over the reference period would be within the limit laid down by the regulations:

$(40 \times 12) + (50 \times 5) = 730. \ 730 \div 17 = 42.94$ hours per week.

For the purpose of calculating the average number of hours worked, certain days are "excluded days". Annual holiday, sick leave, maternity leave and any time during which the employee does not work are excluded days. There is a formula for making the appropriate calculation: A + B - C, where:

- A is the number of hours worked during the reference period;
- B is the number of hours worked in the days added to the end of the reference period to account for days that are excluded; and
- C is the number of weeks making up the reference period.

For example, if a worker works 700 hours during the reference period of seventeen weeks and then works seventy hours during days added due to excluded days, the hours worked are within the prescribed limits:

$700 \ (A) + 70 \ (B) = 770. \ 770 \div 17 \ (C) = 45.29$ hours per week.

The regulations allow individual workers to opt out. The forty-eight hours rule can be disapplied in individual cases, but only if the employee consents and the agreement is in writing. Certain classes of worker are also exempt, but these exemptions have no relevance to clubs.

Holidays and Rest Periods

The Working Time Regulations make provision not only for maximum working hours, but also for regular breaks during working periods and for holidays. The breaks to which an employee is entitled are, in broad terms, as follows. Where an adult worker's daily working time is more than six hours, the worker is entitled to a rest break. In the absence of any collective or workforce agreement, the rest period is twenty minutes. The worker is entitled to spend that period of time away from the usual workstation. Where a worker is employed for periods in excess of six hours, it may be appropriate for the break entitlement to be increased in the light of ongoing health and safety obligations. If a worker is working for, say, nine hours a day, it might be appropriate to have a break of thirty minutes, or two breaks of fifteen minutes each.

All workers who are within the scope of the Working Time Regulations 1998 are entitled to paid annual leave, but only if they have been in continuous employment for a period of thirteen weeks.

Where an employee is entitled to paid leave by virtue of a contract of employment, the leave mentioned in the above paragraph is not an entitlement to additional leave. Any payments made by an employer pursuant to the employee's rights under the regulations goes towards any payments that must be made under the terms of the contract, and *vice versa*.

The European Working Time directive fixed the minimum paid leave entitlement at four weeks in any leave year. That period has applied in the United Kingdom since 23 November 1999 and remains the statutory minimum leave period.

The Leave Year

Employers and employees may agree between themselves when the leave year is to begin. It may be included in the contract of employment and may be determined by the exigencies of the business. In the absence of any such agreement, the leave year is taken to begin on 1 October in the case of a worker whose employment began before 1 October 1998. Otherwise, the leave year begins on the date the employment commenced.

6.   The National Minimum Wage

A minimum wage came into effect on 1 April 1999 when the National Minimum Wage Regulations 1999 (Statutory Instrument 1999 No. 584) came into force. Under the regulations, persons who have attained the qualifying ages are entitled to receive a minimum hourly wage. The regulations give effect to European directives on minimum wages.

With effect from 1 October 2004, the standard national minimum wage is £4.85 per hour. Certain persons, including workers aged between eighteen and twenty-one, qualify for a minimum wage of £4.10 per hour. Workers aged below eighteen who are no longer of compulsory school age qualify for a minimum wage of £3.00 per hour.

The Inland Revenue keeps an eye on minimum wage provisions since it is in a good position to monitor payments and to spot breaches of the regulations. The Inland Revenue may well draw the attention of an offending employer to the regulatory obligations. A worker who is not being paid the correct minimum hourly rate can apply to an industrial tribunal to enforce the correct rate.

An employee who gives up employment because the employer does not pay the minimum wage would have a strong case for constructive dismissal before a tribunal. In addition, since the duty to comply with the regulations may be deemed to be an implied term of a contract of employment, an aggrieved employee may be able to claim in the county court for damages for breach of contract.

7.   Health and Safety

See also Chapter 16, for a club's duty as an employer in respect of health and safety at work, and to conduct risk assessments.

Chapter 13

The Conduct of Members and Guests

1. The Duty of Members and Guests

The members of a members' club have an obligation to conduct themselves in a proper, orderly manner when using the club premises and facilities, and to comply with the law and with the club's rules. Breaches of the law or rules, or behaviour amounting to misconduct, give rise to the possibility of disciplinary action, which may include termination of membership.

Guests of members are expected to conduct themselves in an orderly fashion while on the club's premises. In addition, a member who introduces a guest has a duty to ensure that the guest is of good conduct. Usually, club rules contain provisions relating to the conduct of members and guests. The rules should be consulted when disciplinary issues arise. When making the rules in the first place, care should be taken to ensure that they are clear and unambiguous on this as on other points. The members should decide, in general meeting, the standards of behaviour they expect of members and guests, and their expectations should be set out in the rules. It may be appropriate to set out specific acts or types of conduct that are not allowed on club premises.

2. Penalties for Misconduct

The rules of a members' club may stipulate penalties for breaches of the rules or other misconduct. The penalties may include suspension for a period of time, or expulsion from membership. The imposition of a financial penalty (a fine) is not an option because of the difficulty of arriving at the appropriate penalty for the misconduct in question, and the even greater problem of enforcing payment.

Where the rules set out procedures for suspension or expulsion of undisciplined members, then providing those procedures are complied with, any decision to suspend or expel has the effect of stripping the member of all the rights and privileges of membership, either temporarily or permanently. The club officers are entitled to enforce the ban should the member try to enter the premises and exercise rights of membership.

The conduct of a member while away from the club premises may give rise to the question whether such behaviour can justify suspension or expulsion from membership. Much would depend on the wording of the rules relating to the behaviour of members. There is nothing in law to prevent a club from taking action on the basis of conduct that occurs away from club premises or that is of a type unconnected with the club or its activities. Many clubs adopt a rule that gives the committee the right to take action if the conduct of a member, in the opinion of the committee, renders that person unfit for membership or generally brings the club into disrepute. Such conduct might include conviction for a criminal offence (particularly if it is of the nature of public disorder or dishonesty), persistent refusal to comply with club rules, or rude or offensive behaviour towards staff or other members.

There is nothing in law that would limit the length of a suspension or the duration of an order of expulsion. At the end of a period of suspension the suspended person is entitled to enjoy all the privileges of membership once more. It is for the members to decide whether a person who has been expelled from membership may, at some later time, re-apply for membership, and to incorporate their decision into the club rules. The rules may allow for a rehabilitation period, but they are more likely to provide that a person who has been expelled is not eligible for membership in the future; were readmission to be contemplated after the passage of time, suspension would seem a more sensible penalty in the first place.

3. Procedures

As a general rule, the courts do not interfere with action taken by a club, especially if the procedures are fair and in accordance with the rules. Clubs should, however, be conscious of the principles of natural justice and of the provisions of the Human Rights Act 1998, even though the statute does not apply to private disciplinary procedures. This is because clubs that are run in good faith ought to provide a system for dealing with misconduct that is fair.

The two principles that clubs should strive to uphold are the right to a fair hearing, and that there should be no punishment without law. In the context of a members' club, these principles are upheld if a proper system is established for dealing with allegations of misconduct. Such a system should require notice to be given to the alleged offender of the details of the allegations. The alleged offender should have the opportunity to address the body that adjudicates on the matter. The adjudicating body should be required to notify the accused person of the decision taken in respect of the allegation and the reasons for its findings. Consideration ought also to be given to whether the accused person should have a right of appeal.

The rules of a club should specify who is to deal with allegations of misconduct. In most cases responsibility is given to a group of members appointed for the purpose, or to the management committee. If an appeal system is to be established, it is advisable for the initial hearing to be conducted by a panel of members appointed to deal with disciplinary matters. This would allow for an appeal to the management committee where the member in question is aggrieved by the decision taken by the panel of members. If the initial hearing is before the management committee, any appeal might have to be dealt with by the members in general meeting, which would not be easy to manage.

4. Delegation of Authority

Not every act of misconduct or indiscipline on the part of a member or guest is serious enough to justify disciplinary proceedings. Many incidents consist of breaches of club rules that can simply be drawn to the attention of the offender. Difficulties can arise if the rules of the club do not make clear who has the power to enforce the rules and the duty of members to comply with directions given by that person.

Officers and committee members usually have authority to ensure the club is operated on proper lines and that members comply with the rules. The members elect the officers and the committee members, and the officers and committee members, as a general rule, have authority to deal with breaches of rules and minor incidents of misbehaviour. In some cases it is sensible for enforcement powers to be delegated to others who are in a better position to exercise control on a day-to-day basis. Enforcement powers might, for example, be delegated to the club steward or bar manager.

Where the authority to ensure that club rules are complied with by members and guests has been delegated under the rules, members and guests are under a duty to comply with any request made or instruction given by the person having delegated powers. Failure to do so would amount to an act of misconduct since it would be a breach of club rules. The rules are in place for the benefit of the members generally. On joining the club and accepting the benefits of membership, every member is aware of the rules. Members contract with one another that they accept the rules and continue to be bound by them.

5. Damages Following Disciplinary Action

A question arising from time to time is whether a member who has a grievance about the way club disciplinary procedures have been applied may sue the club for damages. For example, where a member is expelled from membership and believes that the expulsion was not justified, can the member sue the club for the damage claimed to have been suffered as a result of the withdrawal of membership rights?

There are several problems in the concept of a member suing a club. The first is that it is likely that a member would be prohibited from taking action against the club. As a general rule, a members' club has no legal identity. It consists of a body of people who come together for common purposes, thereby forming an unincorporated association. The club's property and other assets are owned by the members in equal shares and so if a member were allowed to sue he would, in effect, be suing himself.

The situation may be different in the case of a club incorporated by shares or guarantee or by virtue of registration under the Industrial and Provident Societies Act 1965. Here there may be a body that has a separate identity and is capable of being sued. It might be said, for example, that the club owes a duty of care to each of its members and that, if a member suffers injury or loss as a consequence of the club's negligence, the member may seek to recover damages.

Even where a club has a separate legal identity, it would be very difficult for a member to obtain damages in respect of a suspension or expulsion. The main problem would be in quantifying the loss. The member might be able to recover any "unused" subscription but otherwise valuing the privileges of membership that have been lost would be far from easy.

As mentioned above, the courts do not usually interfere with matters of club discipline as long as the club rules have been complied with. In agreeing to abide by club rules, a member agrees to accept the authority of the disciplinary panel and abide by any decision it might reach.

6. Guests

Most clubs cater for guests. They may be people brought to the premises by members of the club, or they may be members of affiliated organisations visiting under reciprocal arrangements which allow the use of club facilities. As mentioned at the beginning of this chapter, guests are expected to behave in a proper manner and to comply with club rules. When a guest is on club premises at the invitation of a club member, that member also has a duty to ensure that the guest behaves in an appropriate manner.

From a practical point of view a club would find it virtually impossible to discipline a guest. The officers of the club and the staff are, however, entitled to ask the guest to leave the premises if the guest misbehaves of refuses to comply with club rules. Steps may also be taken to ensure that the offender is not allowed to enter the premises in the future. In extreme cases, the member may be liable to disciplinary action for failing to control the guest.

Most clubs have a rule that limits the number of guests a member may introduce to the club on any single occasion. This rule serves two purposes. First, it ensures that, usually, the persons in attendance are mostly members. This, in turn, means that the members remain in control of their club. Next, the rule serves to demonstrate that the club is properly constituted and run as a members' club, that is, as a club owned by the members and run by them for their collective benefit.

Chapter 14

The Purchase and Supply of Intoxicating Liquor

1. Introduction

It is because clubs wish to be allowed to carry on "qualifying club activities", including the supply of intoxicating liquor, that it is necessary for them to obtain club premises certificates. Groups of like-minded people who meet for social, recreational or educational reasons that do not include the supply of alcohol, the provision of entertainment, gaming or any other qualifying club activity can do so without having to apply for a club premises certificate.

The Licensing Act 2003 contains provisions controlling the purchase of alcohol and its supply.

2. Qualifying Requirements

Under the terms of the Licensing Act 1964, the ways in which alcohol was purchased and the supply of alcohol managed were one of the considerations to be taken into account when determining whether a club qualified for registration. Section 41 of the Act contained the relevant provisions. They have been replicated in sections 63 to 66 of the Act of 2003 which focus on the question whether a club is a qualifying club. Practitioners and club officers who are familiar with the earlier Act will have little difficulty dealing with this aspect of applications under the new legislation.

First, in deciding whether a club is established and conducted in good faith, licensing committees must have regard to any arrangements restricting the club's freedom to purchase alcohol. Any such restriction might indicate an improper interest in the choice of supplier, or arrangements for individuals to receive commission or other payment in respect of alcohol supplied (see also pages 10–11).

Next, there is a requirement that, unless they are managed by the club in general meeting or otherwise by the general body of members, the purchase and supply of alcohol for the club must be managed by a committee whose members are members of the club, over the age of eighteen, who have been elected by members of the club.

The position is slightly different in the case of a club registered under the Industrial and Provident Societies Act 1965 or the Friendly Societies Act 1974, or a registered friendly society within the meaning of the Friendly Societies Act 1992. Such clubs are taken to satisfy this condition if the purchase and supply of alcohol is under the control of a committee of members appointed by the members. This is because, when it became registered in the first place, the club would have had to satisfy the national organisation that it met the statutory requirements to qualify as a *bona fide* members' club.

Special provisions apply to miners' welfare institutes. These institutes are taken automatically to satisfy this condition.

3. Licensing Hours

The Licensing Act 1964 contained restrictions on the hours during which alcohol might be supplied in a members' club. Latterly, clubs were bound by the general permitted hours contained in section 60 of the Act, except on Christmas Day when they could fix their own hours within specified limits.

The Act of 2003 sweeps away the concept of permitted hours, making way for greater freedom of choice. In theory, twenty-four hour supply is possible. There has been much discussion about the wisdom of this change and the effect that it will have on public order, anti-social behaviour and "binge drinking". The concerns are countered by the argument that staggering closing times for different premises will have the effect of evening out the flow of persons leaving premises in busy leisure areas with the consequence that these problems will be alleviated. In practice, it is unlikely that clubs will wish to be allowed to supply alcohol for twenty-four hours. There are real logistical and economic problems that would make such a course of action unlikely.

New Applications

A club applying for a club premises certificate has to decide in advance on the hours during which it wishes to be able to supply alcohol to members and guests. Once a decision has been made, the chosen hours should be set out in the club's operating schedule which is included in the application (see Chapter 4). Subject to any limiting condition that may be imposed by the licensing committee when it determines the application (see pages 30–31), the hours set out in the schedule become the hours during which alcohol may be supplied in that club. Once a club has fixed its hours in this way, the only way it can extend them is by applying for the variation of the club premises certificate (see Chapter 6). On the other hand, the club is not obliged to remain open during all the hours specified in its operating schedule.

The changes introduced by the 2003 Act mean that a club no longer needs to apply for a special order of exemption if it wishes to supply alcohol during additional hours. But when deciding on the hours to be specified in the club operating schedule, account should be taken of special events that may give rise to a need for longer hours. If a club wishes to stage special events on Bank Holidays or arrange award ceremonies or summer balls, it must remember to allow for any additional hours. For example, a club operating schedule may provide for the supply of alcohol between 10 a.m. and midnight as a general rule, but between 10 a.m. and 4 a.m. on Bank Holiday Mondays and on other occasions when award ceremonies or special balls are being held.

Transitional Applications

The situation is different where a club is seeking the conversion of an existing club registration certificate (see Chapter 3). In such cases the hours under the new premises certificate are those that were allowed under the terms of the old certificate and any orders – that is, the permitted hours set out in section 60 of the Licensing Act 1964, as extended by any certificates or special hours orders granted in respect of the premises. Any conditions that were attached to the old certificate apply to the new certificate after conversion. It is clearly important that when applying for the conversion of a certificate, the original certificate and all ancillary certificates and orders are enclosed with it.

An applicant who wishes to be allowed to keep the club premises open for the supply of intoxicants for longer periods than authorised under the 1964 Act will have to apply for the variation of the new premises certificate once it has been granted. The application for variation may be made at the same time as the application for conversion. The licensing authority must then determine the application for conversion before turning its attention to the request for variation.

As mentioned in Chapter 3, there is a dichotomy in the legislation that will give rise to difficulties. Licensing authorities are allowed a period of two months in which to determine an application for the conversion of an existing certificate or for a variation. An application for conversion that has not been dealt with in that time must be treated as having been granted. By contrast, if a licensing authority has not determined an application for variation within the prescribed time limit, the application is to be treated as having been refused. The probability is that there will be many thousands of applications for conversion and variation during the transitional period. The volume of applications may well result in a high proportion of them not being processed within the prescribed time limit. Many applicants are likely to find that their conversion applications are granted by default but that their requests for variation are deemed refused because of the default. They will have no option but to appeal against the refusal. This is a highly unsatisfactory state of affairs.

Guidance on Trading Hours

The Guidance Document published by the Secretary of State under section 182 of the Licensing Act 2003 includes a section on trading hours (section 6). It indicates that, in determining an application by a members' club for a club premises certificate and the hours during which qualifying activities may take place, it is not for the licensing authority to consider such matters as the rights of workers employed at the premises. Other statutes address those issues and give the necessary protection to the workforce. (See Chapter 12). The section goes on to emphasise other principles and government beliefs. The following are extracts taken from the Guidance Document:

> "6.5 The Government strongly believes that fixed and artificially early closing times promote, in the case of the sale or supply of alcohol for consumption on the premises, rapid binge drinking close to closing times, and are a key cause of disorder and disturbance when large numbers of customers [members] are required to leave premises simultaneously . . .

6.10 Licensing authorities should . . . not seek to engineer 'staggered closing times' by setting quotas for particular closing times . . . The general principle should be to support later opening so that customers [members] leave for natural reasons slowly over a longer period.

6.14 . . . there is no obligation under the 2003 Act requiring the holder of a . . . club premises certificate to remain open for the entire period permitted by [the] certificate."

The last extract addresses a concern often raised in relation to the hours that a members' club ought to include in its operating schedule. The inclusion of extended hours that will be required on Bank Holidays or other special occasions such as days on which annual award ceremonies are held, does not commit the club to remaining open to members for the purpose of providing qualifying activities on those or any other days.

4. Supply by Under-age Staff

In Chapter 7, the prohibitions relating to the supply to and consumption of alcohol by young persons are examined. Section 153 of the Licensing Act 2003 focuses on the supply of alcohol *by* persons who have not attained the age of eighteen. Supply by a person under eighteen is not totally banned, but no person under that age can supply intoxicating liquor by or on behalf of a club or to the order of a member of the club unless the supply has been specifically approved by a responsible person.

A "responsible person" means any member or officer of the club present on the premises in a capacity which enables that person to prevent the supply in question.

The prohibition imposed by section 153 does not apply where alcohol is supplied for consumption with a table meal, in premises, or part of premises, which are being used for the service of table meals. For this exception to apply, the premises, or the relevant part of them, must not be in use for the supply of alcohol otherwise than to persons taking tables meals there and for consumption by such persons as an ancillary to their meals.

These provisions allow a person under the age of eighteen to supply alcohol in the club's bar on behalf of the club, but only if the supply is specifically authorised by a responsible person. It seems, however, that a person under the age of eighteen may work in any part of the club's premises set apart for the service of table meals and supply alcohol on behalf of the club without specific authorisation, as long as the person to whom it is supplied is having a meal and the drinks are ancillary to that meal.

5. Smuggled Goods

The relaxation of import controls following European Community agreements have made it possible for unscrupulous people to bring large quantities of alcohol into the country with the object of selling it on to pubs, clubs and off-licences. Much publicised "booze cruises" are the source of many of these illegal operations. Club officers should exercise extreme caution to avoid the possibility of purchasing any such smuggled goods. It is a serious offence to keep smuggled goods on club premises.

Section 144 of the Licensing Act provides that the offence is committed if any person knowingly keeps, or allows to be kept, on any relevant premises, any goods which have been imported without payment of duty or which have otherwise been unlawfully imported. In the case of premises that have the benefit of a club premises certificate, any member or officer of the club present on the premises when smuggled goods are kept there, in a capacity that enables the member or officer to prevent them from being so kept, may be charged with the offence. The maximum penalty is a fine not exceeding £1,000.

Chapter 15

Entertainment

1. Introduction

Until the Licensing Act 2003 is fully in force, a members' club which provides public entertainment has first to apply to the local authority for the relevant area for a certificate of suitability. Under the new legislation, a club that wishes, or may wish, to provide regulated entertainment should, when applying for a club premises certificate, or to convert an existing club registration certificate, include the relevant entertainment(s) in the list of qualifying activities to be allowed under the club premises certificate.

Schedule 1 to the Licensing Act 2003 concerns the provision of regulated entertainment or entertainment facilities, either exclusively for members of a qualifying club, or for the members of such a club or their guests.

The entertainments within the provisions of the schedule are:
- a performance of a play;
- an exhibition of a film;
- an indoor sporting event;
- a boxing or wrestling entertainment;
- a performance of live music;
- any playing of recorded music;
- a performance of dance;
- live music, recorded music or dance which takes place in the presence of an audience and is provided wholly or partly to entertain that audience.

The entertainment facilities within the schedule are:
- making music;
- dancing; and
- other similar entertainment.

2. Transitional Applications

A club that wishes to take advantage of the transitional provisions set out in the Licensing Act 2003 and described in Chapter 3 should apply for the conversion of its existing club registration certificate to a club premises certificate. When making the application, care should be taken to include all existing club activities which are to be treated as qualifying activities under the new Act and so to be authorised under the new certificate. The provision of entertainment is such an activity.

When submitting the application, the club should make sure that the original registration certificate is attached, together with the existing certificate of suitability (and any other documents that may be relevant, such as supper hour certificates or special hours orders). If the certificate of suitability is not enclosed, the provision of entertainment will not be included in the qualifying activities that are authorised by the converted club premises certificate.

See Chapter 3 for more detail on transitional applications.

3. New Applications

In the case of a members' club applying for a new club premises certificate after the 2003 Act has come into full force, the provision of entertainment should be included as a qualifying activity which the club wishes to be allowed to engage in, when the club operating schedule is completed. The activities specified in the schedule will, as a general rule, be translated into the permitted qualifying activities authorised under the certificate. If the provision of entertainment is not included, an application for the variation of the club premises certificate will have to be made should the club wish, subsequently, to provide it. See Chapter 4 for a more detailed explanation of the procedure for new applications.

4. Licences to use Copyright Works

Clubs which provide entertainment by live performers, discotheques, electronic reproduction of sound such as by compact discs, television or a juke box, are not free to provide that entertainment simply because they have a certificate of suitability or a club premises certificate. Copyright licences may have to be obtained and fees paid to the organisations that look after the interests of the artistes responsible for the creation of such entertainment and those who produce it and have copyright interests in the material. The bodies in question are the Performing Right Society and Phonographic Performance Ltd. Many clubs provide entertainment illegally, simply because they do not know about their obligations to pay fees to these two bodies.

The function of the Performing Right Society is to safeguard the rights of composers and lyricists in relation to the public performance of their works. The Society levies fees for the right to give such public performances and the fees raised are distributed to those who produced the music or songs performed. Several different tariffs apply, depending on how the copyright material is used. Members' clubs come within a tariff known as the Joint Members' Clubs ("JMC") tariff.

The fees charged change from time to time. At the time of writing, the JMC tariff in force is effective from 1 August 2004 to 31 July 2005. It applies to performances of copyright music within the Society's repertoire at clubs *bona fide* established and conducted in good faith as non-profit-making members' clubs capable of registration under Part II of the Licensing Act 1964. It does not apply to proprietary clubs.

If a club applies for and obtains the Society's licence before musical performances commence, the standard royalty rate is payable in respect of the first year of the licence. If the music user does not obtain a licence before musical performances commence, the higher royalty rate (standard plus 50 per cent) is payable for the first year of the licence. In either case, at the end of the first year, the standard royalty rate is charged and payable.

The current rates are as follows. See pages 111–113 for definitions of the terms used:

Live music
Where the club's annual expenditure on providing music by performers is £6,788 or more, the standard royalty is 2.5 per cent of the club's actual annual expenditure. The higher rate is 3.75 per cent of such expenditure.

Where annual expenditure on providing live music is less than £6,788, the royalty per function, for the first 100 persons capacity, for performances of music by performers in person is £3.43 (standard royalty) or £5.13 (higher rate royalty). For each additional twenty-five persons capacity, or part of such number, an additional £0.86

(standard royalty) or £1.29 (higher rate royalty) is payable. The total annual fee is, however, capped at £169.70 (standard royalty) or £254.55 (higher rate royalty).

Featured Recorded Music

For all performances by record, compact disc or tape player primarily for entertainment by means of discotheque equipment or otherwise for dancing and karaoke performances, the standard royalty for the first 100 persons present is £3.44 and the higher rate is £5.13. For each additional twenty-five persons, or part of such number, the royalty is £0.86 (standard rate) and £1.29 (higher rate). But where performances of this type are given at a function, and in the same room where performances are also given in person and in respect of which royalties are paid, the rates are reduced to £1.67 or £2.51 for the first 100 people; and £0.42 or £0.63 per additional twenty-five people.

Annual Licence for Featured Music

The minimum royalty for an annual licence for featured music under this tariff is £84.85 (standard royalty) or £127.28 (higher rate). Where, however, there are no more than three functions in a licence year, these minimum rates are not charged. In such cases, the charge for each function is a minimum of £21.21 (standard royalty) or £31.82 (higher rate).

Cinema and Featured Video

For showing films or videos in a room or place specially used for video or cinema exhibition, and with seating arranged accordingly, the royalty charged for the first 100 people in attendance is £1.67 (standard rate) or £2.51 (higher rate). The additional payment per twenty-five people is £0.42 (standard rate) and £0.63 (higher rate).

Background or Mechanical Music

The annual royalties are as follows:

Television (without video)
- screen no larger than 26 inches (66 cms): £70.72 (standard rate) or £106.08 (higher rate);
- screen larger than 26 inches (66 cms): £106.06 (standard rate) or £159. 09 (higher rate).

Radio: £70.72 (standard rate) or £106.08 (higher rate), per set.

Video player (with or without television facilities through the same screen) except performances where there are special seating arrangements for viewing, or when the player is used for discotheque performances:

- screen no larger than 26 inches (66 cms): £106.06 (standard rate) or £159.09 (higher rate) per player;
- screen larger than 26 inches (66 cms): £141.45 (standard rate) or £212.18 (higher rate) per player.

Record, compact disc or tape player, or music centre: £155.60 (standard rate) or £233.40 (higher rate) per player. Where two or more such instruments or screens are used in the same premises, whether of the same or of different kinds, the combined charges for the instruments is reduced by 10 per cent.

Jukeboxes:
Audio jukebox: £175.53 (standard rate) or £263.30 (higher rate).
Audio jukebox with background music facility: £247.12 (standard rate) or £370.68 (higher rate).
Video jukebox:

- screen no larger than 26 inches (66 cms): £230.98 (standard rate) or £346.47 (higher rate);.
- screen larger than 26 inches (66 cms): £277.19 (standard rate) or £415.79 (higher rate).

Video jukebox with background music facility:

- screen no larger than 26 inches (66 cms): £286.41 (standard rate) or £429.62 (higher rate);
- screen larger than 26 inches (66 cms): £321.07 (standard rate) or £481.61 (higher rate).

Combined audio/video jukebox with background music facility

- screen no larger than 26 inches (66 cms): £316.43 (standard rate) or £474.65 (higher rate);
- screen larger than 26 inches (66 cms): £345.37 (standard rate) or £518.06 (higher rate).

For each additional coin entry point (jukeboxes) an additional charge of £23.10 (standard rate) or £34.65 (higher rate) is made.
Value added tax is payable on all royalties charged.

Definitions
Terms used in the scale of royalties set out above are defined as follows:

- *annual expenditure on the provision of music*: the total of gross wages, fees, expenses or other emoluments paid to performers (excluding any disc jockeys) and gross fees (net of VAT) paid to third parties for the services of performers;

- *audio jukebox*: a machine (other than a video jukebox) for playing recorded music, capable of being operated by the insertion of a coin, token or card;

- *audio jukebox with background music facility, or video jukebox with background music facility, or combined audio/ video jukebox with background music facility, or music centre and/or radio cassette player*: a combination of units of equipment capable of reproducing sound from more than one source through a single sound system;

- *background or mechanical music*: music when performed by a record player, compact disc player, tape player, or video player otherwise than for featured purposes, or music performed by a radio or television set operated on the premises or diffused through a loud speaker from another part of the premises or a source outside the premises;

- *featured music or featured recorded music*: music performed by performers in person or a record, compact disc or tape player primarily for entertainment by means of discotheque equipment or otherwise for dancing or in conjunction with cabaret or similar entertainment, or cinematograph equipment or video player;

- *karaoke performance*: performances given by unpaid singers in conjunction with specially produced recorded music, with or without the provision of video-presented synchronised lyrics;

- *music centre*: instruments combining a radio and tape player and/or record player;

- *performers*: singers and performers of musical instruments, including orchestral conductors and leaders, whether or not they combine in their performance other activities such as dancing or acting as comperes;

- *record, compact disc or tape player*: any gramophone, compact disc, tape or cassette player or other mechanical/ electronic contrivance for playing musical works, except: a video player, or contrivance such as a jukebox, capable of being operated by the insertion of a coin, token or card;

- *the Society's repertoire*: all and any musical works (including any words associated herewith), the right of public performance of which is controlled by the Performing Right Society or by any of the societies in other countries with which the Society is affiliated;

• *video jukebox*: a machine for playing recorded music synchronised with a video or similar visual display and capable of being operated by the insertion of a coin, token or card.

"Capacity" is calculated as follows: where the accommodation of a room is limited to the number of seats, the capacity is calculated by reference to the total number of seats. Where, as in the case of discotheque performances, there is no formal means of calculating the accommodation of a room, capacity is assessed by reference to the maximum number of persons who can reasonably be accommodated in the room, or which is permitted under any regulation by the fire authority of under the club's rules. Where the capacity exceeds 100 persons, one quarter of the charge is levied on each twenty-five persons.

Forms of application for licences are obtainable from the Society whose offices are at 29-33 Berners Street, London W1P 4AA. Advice can be obtained by telephone on 020 7580 5544. Its website address is www.prs.co.uk. Arrangements can also be made for Society inspectors to visit club premises to assess the club's needs and advise on appropriate fees. Inspectors are able to issue licences at the time of visiting.

Clubs which provide musical entertainment may also have to obtain a licence from Phonographic Performance Ltd ("PPL"). This may seem strange when fees are also payable to the Performing Right Society, but there are two quite separate copyrights in each sound recording. The songwriter or composer owns the copyright in the song, and licence fees in respect of that copyright are collected by the Performing Right Society. The copyright in the *recording* is owned by the record company which financed and produced it, and its licence fees are collected by PPL.

PPL levies its fees in advance. This is because permission must be obtained before the performance takes place. Once the appropriate fee has been paid, PPL issues its licence fairly quickly. The fee payable is based entirely on the information the applicant provides about its public use of sound recordings. Once PPL has that information, it determines which of its charging tariffs is appropriate.

The company says that by relating licence fees very specifically to the actual use made of sound recordings, it can ensure that the applicant is not overcharged.

PPL has its offices at 1, Upper James Street, London W1F 9DE and advice can be obtained from the company by telephone on 020 7534 1000. The company's website address is www. ppluk.com

5. Film and Television Screening

Films

Great care has to be taken by a members' club wishing to screen films for members and guests. First, before it may exhibit a film on the club premises, the club's premises certificate must include the exhibition of films as one of the qualifying activities. Where the certificate does authorise the exhibition of films, the authorisation must be subject to the condition that restricts the admission of children in accordance with section 74 of the Licensing Act 2003. That section provides that if a "film classification body" (in effect, the British Board of Film Classification) is specified in the certificate, admission must, generally, be restricted in accordance with any recommendation made by the Board. For example, if a film is classified as a film for exhibition to persons over the age of fifteen, children under that age may not be admitted to the performance. If the British Board of Film Classification is not specified in the premises certificate, or the licensing authority has notified the club that admission is to be restricted in accordance with any recommendation made by the authority itself, then the authority's own restrictions, if any, must be respected. For example, if the authority has applied an "eighteen" classification to the film, persons under that age must be excluded.

Some thought must also be given to the source of the films that are to be shown. Films that are rented or purchased from a retail outlet cannot be shown. Copyright laws restrict the screening of such films to the home. Films may be screened for the members of a club only if they have been obtained from a non-theatrical distributor who provides the club with a copyright licence.

Care must also be taken to ensure that the club is not acting as a "cinema". The films that are shown in the club must not be advertised outside the premises and the general public must not be admitted to performances of the film in return for an entrance fee.

The Federation Against Copyright Theft ("FACT") acts as the regulating body for the film industry. It monitors activities such as piracy and illegal screenings. Prosecutions arising from investigations by this body can lead to the imposition of substantial fines.

Further information about the screening of films in members' clubs can be obtained from FACT who have offices at 7 Victory Business Centre, Worton Road, Isleworth, Middlesex TW7 6DB. The telephone number is 020 8568 6646 and the website address is www.fact-uk.org.uk.

Information about hiring films for screening in club premises can be obtained from Filmbank Distributors Ltd, 98 Theobalds Road, London WC1X 8WB; telephone 020 7984 5958; www.filmbank. co.uk.

Television Programmes

The simultaneous reception and playing of a television programme does not constitute "regulated entertainment" for the purposes of the Licensing Act. Members' clubs should, though, exercise caution when contemplating screening televised programmes such as major sporting events. To receive transmissions from terrestrial television companies the club must have a television licence for its premises. In the case of satellite transmissions, the club needs the appropriate authority from the satellite broadcasting company.

Sky Television issues viewing cards that authorise the reception of its transmissions. The company does not issue the same cards for all types of premises. Organisations such as members' clubs are not allowed to screen transmissions using a viewing card sold to an individual member. The charge Sky makes for authority to receive transmissions depends on the programme(s) in question. Details of the fees that would be charged to a members' club can be supplied by Sky TV; www.business.sky.com. Fees generally reflect the appeal of the programmes that are to be shown and the size of the potential audience.

6. Plays

Some clubs may have occasion to stage plays on club premises. Once again, a club that wishes, or may wish, to do so should include this activity in the club operating schedule submitted with the application for a club premises certificate. The performance of plays will then be included as one of the club's qualifying activities.

Section 76 of the Licensing Act provides that the licensing authority may impose conditions on the certificate in relation to the performance of plays only if it considers it necessary to do so in the interests of public safety. Conditions might, for example, prohibit the use of naked flames during productions, or the number of persons who might appear on stage at any one time. The type of play to be performed, or the content of the plays, may not be the subject of conditions attaching to the premises certificate.

7. Bingo and Other Gaming

A members' club that wishes to use its premises for gaming must, for the time being, apply for registration under Part II of the Gaming Act 1968. Gaming is not a regulated entertainment for the purposes of the Licensing Act 2003 and, consequently, it is not a qualifying activity.

Application for registration must, broadly speaking, follow the procedures set out in Schedule 2 to the 1968 Act.

The application must be sent to the chief executive of the gaming committee having jurisdiction over the area in which the premises are situated, that is, the chief executive of the local magistrates' court. The application must be in the prescribed form (see Appendix A). It must specify the name and description of the club and other prescribed particulars.

Not later than seven days after the application is submitted, a copy of it must be sent to the chief officer of police for the area in which the premises are situated, and to the Collector of Customs and Excise for that area. Not later than fourteen days after the application is submitted, the club must advertise the application to the public, in a newspaper that circulates in the gaming committee's area.

As long as the paper does circulate in the relevant area, it does not have to be a local newspaper: *R v Westminster Betting Licensing Committee, ex parte Peabody Donation Fund Governors*. This case applies to press advertisements of applications made under the Gaming Act 1968 even though there is some doubt whether it applies to applications made under the Licensing Act 2003 (see page 28).

Members' clubs are not required to post a notice of the application outside the entrance to its premises or to serve a copy of the application on the local authority or the fire authority.

Chapter 16

Liability to Members and to the Public

1. Introduction

Those responsible for the management of a members' club need to be fully aware of the club's responsibilities in respect of the safety and well-being of members, guests and others who may come onto, or into the vicinity of, the club's premises. All clubs have obligations under the common law and statute law in relation to the safety and well-being of such people; and clubs which provide food on club premises also have responsibilities in relation to food hygiene. All clubs should ensure these responsibilities are understood. They should carry out regular risk assessments and ensure that the club has an adequate level of insurance to guard against any compensation or damages which the club may be ordered to pay if a claim is successfully made against it. Risk assessment is covered in more detail later in this chapter.

2. The Duty of Care to Members and Guests

As the owner and occupier of the club's premises, the club is under a duty to ensure the safety of persons who have its permission or authority to be on those premises. The duty is owed to members and guests, and to other persons, such as tradesmen and visiting team members who come onto the premises by licence or specific invitation.

The general duty of care had its origins in the common law, although the common law provisions are now enacted in the Occupiers' Liability Act 1957. Thus, the persons who, for the purposes of the Act, are treated as an occupier and his visitors are, generally, the same as the persons who would be treated as an

117

occupier and as his invitees or licensees.

The general duty is to take such care as is, in all the circumstances, reasonable, to see that a visitor to the premises will be reasonably safe in using them for the purposes for which he is invited or permitted by the occupier to be there.

For the purposes of the Occupiers' Liability Act, members and guests are treated as visitors since they are persons who come onto the club premises at the invitation of the club.

When assessing liability, the degree to which a visitor exercises care in relation to his or her own safety is one of the circumstances to be taken into account. In this respect, the occupier:

- must be prepared for children to be less careful than adults; and
- may expect that a person, in the exercise of that person's calling, will appreciate and guard against any special risks ordinarily incident to it, so far as the occupier leaves the person free to do so. For example, an electrician is taken to be aware of the dangers of electrical installations, and a roofing contractor is taken to appreciate the risks of working on high, and possibly fragile, structures.

Particular note should be taken of the fact that the law recognises that children are less likely to have regard for their own safety than adults. Courts may find that dangers that would be clear and obvious to adults may be considered concealed hazards as far as children are concerned. Special care should therefore be taken in relation to anything that might be especially tempting or alluring to young children, such as turnstiles, escalators, pools or other areas of unguarded water.

Parents of younger members and guests are not absolved from their parental obligations. A club may be found to have discharged its duty of care towards a child if it gave notice to parents of any obvious danger that might be encountered on the premises, and the warning was given in a form that would be easily understood by the parents.

To succeed in a claim for damages or compensation for injuries suffered on club premises, the claimant would have to satisfy the court that the club had, in some way, failed in its duty of care. If the club is able to show that it took all reasonable precautions to guard against the risk of injury and to prevent members and guests from coming to harm it will be in a strong position to contest any claim.

Whether the precautions taken were reasonable, in all the circumstances, would be a matter for a court to decide on the facts.

Certain steps, however, go a long way to countering any claim for negligence. First, clubs should take the precaution of carrying out regular risk assessments. The club premises should be examined to identify any hazardous features of the property which should be guarded against, if not removed. The findings of these risk assessments should be recorded, as should the steps taken to remove or minimise each risk. Production of such a record would be of great assistance in any proceedings that might be brought. Risk assessment is considered in greater depth later in this chapter.

Another precaution a club might reasonably take would be to post warning notices, that cannot easily be eradicated, in conspicuous places adjacent to any hazard. Clearly exhibiting a notice that draws attention to a hazard or disclaims liability for injuries caused by it would not, in itself, exonerate the club from liability for injury or damage caused by it, but it may considerably reduce the club's liability if a claim for compensation were made. If it can be shown that the club has been negligent in any way or otherwise failed in its duty of care, it may still be held liable and ordered to pay damages or compensation to the claimant.

Generally, it is advisable to post warning and disclaimer notices where appropriate, because their presence will make it more difficult, if a claim is made, to show that the club was negligent. Even if a degree of negligence is proved, such warnings may well mitigate the extent of the club's liability.

3.   The Duty of Care to Non-members

A club's duty to safeguard members and guests has been discussed above. A club also has a general duty as the occupier of premises to prevent harm to others who may come onto the premises. The duty of care extends to predictable harm that may be caused to persons outside club premises as a result of the activities that take place on the premises.

Many people, other than members or guests, have occasion to come onto a club's premises. Workmen, trades people, representatives of retailers or wholesalers, visiting entertainers and members of visiting sports teams may all visit the premises from time to time. All these people are visitors for the purposes of the

Occupiers' Liability Act 1957 and the club, as occupier of the premises, has a duty of care in respect of them. Accordingly, it must take all reasonable steps to ensure such persons do not come to harm as a result of the condition of the premises or any activity carried out on the premises. In certain circumstances, the duty of care may extend to persons who find themselves in the vicinity of the club's premises.

It may be difficult to accept the proposition that a club, as occupier of its premises, has a duty of care to persons who venture onto them unlawfully, but the law does extend the duty of care to such persons. It may not be as onerous in the case of trespassers, but obvious dangers should be guarded against. A good example of the fact that it is necessary to safeguard trespassers from predictable harm may be found in the warnings frequently posted on premises guarded by dogs at night.

An occupier's duty in respect of persons other than visitors is set out in the Occupiers' Liability Act 1984. This Act provides that an occupier owes a duty of care to persons other than visitors in respect of certain specified risks. These are the risks of suffering injury on the premises by reason of any danger due to the state of the premises, or to things done or omitted to be done on them. Liability arises if:

- the occupier is aware of the danger or has reasonable grounds to believe that it exists;
- the occupier knows or has reasonable grounds to believe that the other is in the vicinity of the danger concerned, or that that other may come into the vicinity of the danger, whether or not that person has lawful authority to be in that vicinity; and
- the risk is one against which, in all the circumstances of the case, the occupier may reasonably be expected to offer the other person some protection.

It is these provisions that bring trespassers and persons who may be passing the club premises within the scope of the occupier's duty of care.

The extent of the occupier's liability is to take such care as is reasonable in all the circumstances to see that the person does not suffer injury by reason of the danger concerned.

The liability which a club may have in respect of damage, injury or loss suffered by persons outside the premises has already been mentioned. The common law duty of care applies and, consequently, it is incumbent on all clubs to examine their activities and to take steps to protect passers-by from any risks from those activities. If it can be shown that the damage or injury suffered was caused by the club's negligence, the club will be liable.

Where, for example, the access road to club premises passes over a public footpath, the surface of the access road should be maintained in a good state of repair. Otherwise, an injury caused if a passer-by stumbles or falls on a damaged or uneven surface may give rise to an order for the payment of compensation. Other examples of potential danger include damage or injury caused by a golf or cricket ball, struck on club premises, striking a passer-by or a passing vehicle.

The Occupiers' Liability Act may come into play in other circumstances. An obvious example is where masonry, or other fixtures forming part of club premises, causes damage or injury by falling into the street because of inadequate maintenance.

4. Noise

Clubs which include among their qualifying activities the provision of musical and other entertainment should ensure that the noise emanating from their premises is controlled at an acceptable level. The effect of noise from club activities on people who live and work in the vicinity of the premises may lead to intervention by environmental health officers.

Noise is one of the pollutants referred to in the Control of Pollution Act 1974. Local authority environmental health officers have power under the Act to take action if they believe that noise emanating from any premises has reached such a level as to constitute a statutory noise nuisance. Most authorities operate a twenty-four hour emergency service that provides for an officer of the authority to respond to complaints about excessive noise at any time of the day or night.

A local authority may serve a notice (an abatement notice) on any person whom it considers to be responsible for a noise nuisance, if it appears that the noise level emanating from premises is not acceptable and that a reduction of the level is practicable at reasonable cost and would afford a public benefit.

A local authority is empowered under the Control of Pollution Act to designate an area as a noise abatement zone. If it does so, it must keep a register of all measurements of noise levels emanating from premises in that area. The level of noise recorded in the register in respect of any premises may not be exceeded unless the local authority has given its written consent. If the noise coming from premises exceeds this level, the person responsible (in the case of a members' club, the chairman or secretary) is guilty of an offence. The penalty is a fine not exceeding £5,000, together with a daily fine of £50 for each day on which the offence continues after the date of the conviction.

5.   Duties as an Employer
In addition to its duties as an occupier of premises, a club usually also has duties because of its position as an employer of staff. Every employer has a duty, under the Health and Safety at Work etc Act 1974, to ensure, so far as is reasonably practicable, the health, safety and welfare at work of all its employees.

Having set out the general duty, the Act goes on to specify certain duties in particular:
- the duty to ensure that any plant provided is properly maintained and that systems for carrying out work are safe and do not give rise to risk to the employee's health;
- the duty to make arrangements in connection with the use, handling, storage and transport of articles and substances that will ensure the safety of staff and the absence of risk of injury to their health;
- the duty to provide proper information, instruction, training and supervision;
- the duty to maintain the employee's place of work in a safe and risk-free condition; and
- the duty to provide a safe and risk-free working environment.

To fulfil these obligations, a club employing staff may have to provide information and training in respect of the potential dangers to people other than its own employees who may work on the club premises from time to time. This is because the Act imposes a duty on the employer to conduct the undertaking so as to ensure, as far as is reasonably practicable, that persons not in his employment who may be affected thereby are not exposed to risks to their health and safety. The cases of *R v Swan Hunter Shipbuilders Ltd* and *R v Board of Trustees of the Science Museum* are relevant. The latter case seems to suggest that in prosecutions arising from this statutory obligation, it is sufficient for the prosecution to prove that members of the public were exposed to a possibility of danger.

The legislation also embraces the responsibilities that most people would expect employees to have in safeguarding their own health and welfare. It provides that employees are under a general duty to:

- take reasonable care for their own safety and for the safety of any other person who may be affected by the employee's acts or omissions while at work; and
- co-operate with the employer as far as is necessary to enable the employer to comply with the duties under the Act.

6. Risk Assessment

To comply with the common law and statutory obligations to those who visit or work in a club's premises, and with the club's duties to other people who may come onto those premises or may otherwise be affected by club activities, officers and committee members need to be fully aware of the nature and extent of the risks that exist at the premises.

The statutory body with responsibility for overseeing health and safety matters is the Health and Safety Executive. It publishes a number of very helpful publications containing advice on a wide range of safety matters. In addition, if a club were to get into difficulties in assessing risks at its premises, the local health and safety inspector is on hand to give advice. Among the publications available from the executive are:

- *Essentials of Health and Safety at Work*;
- *Management of Health and Safety at Work*; and
- *Writing your Health and Safety Policy Statement.*

The executive also supplies a number of helpful booklets containing advice expressed in straightforward language. They include:

- *An Introduction to Health and Safety*; and
- *Five Steps to Risk Assessment.*

The five topics addressed in the latter booklet are:

- looking for hazards;
- deciding who might be harmed, and how;
- evaluating the risks arising from the hazards and deciding whether existing precautions are adequate;
- recording findings, and

• reviewing and revising assessments.

The following extracts give a flavour of the guidance contained in the document:

"... walk around your workplace [club premises] and look afresh at what could reasonably be expected to cause harm... Ask your employees or their representatives what they think...

Decide who might be harmed and how. Don't forget . . . cleaners, visitors, contractors, maintenance contractors etc who may not be in the workplace all the time...

What you have to decide for each significant hazard is whether the remaining risk is high, medium or low. First ask yourself whether you have done all the things that the law says you have got to do...

In taking action ask yourself, a) can I get rid of the hazard altogether? b) if not, how can I control the risks so that harm is unlikely? . . .

If you have fewer than five employees you do not need to write anything down . . . but if you employ five or more people you must record the significant findings of your assessment. This means writing down the significant hazards and conclusions...

You need to be able to show that a proper check was made, you asked who might be affected, you dealt with all the obvious significant hazards . . ., the precautions are reasonable and the remaining risk is low."

The Health and Safety Executive has an information hotline: 08701 545 500. Its website address is www.hse.gov.uk.

7.   The Supply of Food

Introduction

Clubs which sell food to members and guests must be aware of their obligations under the Food Safety Act 1990 and related regulations on food hygiene. The Department of Health advises that anyone who owns, manages or works in a food business is affected by the regulations, whether they sell publicly or privately, in a hotel or marquee, for profit or for fund-raising. Generally, anyone who handles food or whose actions could affect its safety must follow the regulations. On the basis of this advice, it is clear that any members' club that provides food must comply with the regulations.

The Food Safety Act 1990

The Food Safety Act 1990 applies to anyone who sells food for human consumption, or who offers, exposes, advertises, or is in possession of food for sale. Failure to meet its requirements is an offence.

It is also an offence to sell food which is not of the nature, substance or quality demanded by the purchaser.

The maximum penalty which may be imposed in the magistrates' court, in respect of each of these offences, is a fine not exceeding £20,000, or a period of imprisonment not exceeding six months, or both. If a person is convicted of this offence in the Crown Court, the maximum term of imprisonment which may be imposed is two years. The maximum fine is four times higher than the usual maximum for a single offence, and is an indication of the seriousness of these offences.

The Act also creates an offence of falsely describing or presenting food. Great care should be taken to see that when food or drink is sold or offered for sale it is described accurately. The maximum penalty is a fine not exceeding £5,000.

A club which is a corporate body may be prosecuted independently of any prosecution that may be brought against its secretary, chairman or other officer.

If a person sells food which is not of the proper nature, substance or quality, or falsely describes or presents food, because of an act or default of some other person, that other person is also guilty of an offence and may be charged with it and convicted, whether or not proceedings are taken against the first person. Consequently, if a club commits one of these offences because of an act or default by its bar steward, both the club and the bar steward may be prosecuted.

The legislation does provide for a statutory defence, although generally it is thought that the offence is one of absolute or strict liability. See the cases of *Betts v Armstead, Winter v Hinckley and District Industrial Co-operative Society Ltd* and *Goodfellow v Johnson*. The defence is to prove (on the balance of probabilities) that the defendant took all reasonable precautions and exercised all due diligence to avoid committing the offence, or to avoid the commission of the offence by a person under the defendant's control.

A person charged with either of these two offences, who neither prepared the food in question nor imported it into Great Britain, establishes the statutory defence by proving:

- that the commission of the offence was due to an act or default of another person who was not under the defendant's control, or to reliance on information supplied by such a person;
- that the defendant carried out all such checks of the food as were reasonable in all the circumstances, or that it was reasonable to rely on checks carried out by the person who supplied the food, and
- that the defendant did not know and had no reason to suspect at the time of the alleged offence that the act or omission would amount to an offence.

This provision could be important where the food complained about was not prepared in the club but bought in from an outside supplier.

A club which intends to rely on a statutory defence as described above must serve on the prosecutor a notice in writing giving whatever information it has in its possession identifying or assisting with the identification of the other person. The notice must be given at least seven clear days before the hearing, but where the club has previously appeared before a court in connection with the alleged offence, it must give the notice within one month of its first such appearance. The purpose of the notice is to give the prosecuting authority the opportunity to check the details given. The notice may result in the prosecution of the supplier and the withdrawal of the case against the club.

Whether or not food is unfit for human consumption is largely a question of fact in each case. The fact that a food inspector used statutory powers to condemn food is not conclusive proof that it was unfit for human consumption, although such condemnation would be strong evidence that it was. See the case of *Waye v Thompson*.

The Regulations

Many regulations have been made under the Food Safety Act. Of greatest interest to clubs that sell food are the Food Safety (General Food Hygiene) Regulations 1995, Statutory Instrument 1995 No. 1763. They contain, among other provisions, general requirements for food premises and specific requirements for rooms where foodstuffs are prepared.

The provisions that relate to food premises generally include requirements concerning:

- the cleanliness of the premises;
- the design and condition of the premises;

- lavatories and washbasins; and
- hand-washing equipment.

They also deal with:

- ventilation of the premises generally;
- ventilation of sanitary conveniences;
- lighting;
- drainage; and
- changing facilities for staff.

The specific provisions concerning food preparation rooms include requirements in relation to:

- floor surfaces;
- wall surfaces;
- ceilings and overhead fixings;
- windows and other openings;
- doors;
- work surfaces;
- the cleaning of equipment; and
- the washing of food.

Some of these points are dealt with in greater detail in the paragraphs that follow.

Risk Assessment

The need for clubs to carry out regular risk assessments in the context of health and safety has already been mentioned (see above). Such assessments are just as important in relation to a club's obligations under food safety legislation. All hazards should be identified; any which are critical to food safety should be given special consideration. A club may conclude that such issues cannot be left to the subjective judgement of its own officers and that a specialist should be called in to carry out the risk assessment.

The local authority may provide a useful point of initial contact. The environmental health departments of local authorities are responsible for monitoring establishments which sell food to ensure that food hygiene regulations are complied with. Many publish their own guides to setting up a food business. A club that wishes to sell food is well advised to contact the local environmental health officer, who will be pleased to offer guidance and may be able to provide helpful literature.

When carrying out food hygiene risk assessments, a club should adopt a systematic approach, focusing on potential hazards as well as hazards that are immediately obvious, every aspect of the food business and working practices, as well as working conditions. The operation should be looked at from the purchase of supplies or ingredients through to the service of food to members and guests; in respect of every point in the procedure, the question whether there is any actual or potential hazard should be posed. If any hazard is identified, the club should go on to see what controls are in place, or should be put in place, to guard against the risk(s) identified.

Some of the works that may need to be put in hand before a club could provide food safely are comparatively simple and inexpensive. In other cases, they may be substantial and costly. Clubs should consider the cost of complying with food hygiene regulations before embarking on catering for the first time. It may be that a club has to accept that it cannot undertake the sale or supply of food because of financial considerations.

The Regulations in Greater Detail
A study of the Food Safety (General Food Hygiene) Regulations shows that, when establishing an acceptable system for the preparation and handling of food, particular attention needs to be given to:

- the construction of the premises being used, their size, layout and design, to be sure that the premises are capable of accommodating the intended procedures safely. Walls and working surfaces must be easily cleaned and regularly maintained;
- the available sanitary and hand-washing facilities and their location. Separate facilities should be available to staff, and their lavatories must not give direct access to food preparation rooms. Hot and cold running water must be available and soap and suitable hand-drying facilities must be available. The staff hand-washing facilities should be separate from the facilities provided for the purpose of washing food; and
- ventilation and lighting. There has to be suitable and sufficient natural and mechanical ventilation, and mechanical systems must be accessible for cleaning and replacing filters. Adequate natural or artificial lighting must also be available.

Generally, all food storage and preparation areas, all processing and cooking equipment and utensils, all ventilation and lighting installations and all sanitary installations must be kept clean, to prevent possible contamination of the food being prepared and supplied.

Microbiological, chemical and physical hazards need to be assessed. The following are examples of these types of hazard:

- contamination caused by bacteria present in food when it is purchased, or which may get into food during preparation processes;
- contamination as a result of cleaning chemicals or materials getting into food;
- contamination as a result of pests or foreign bodies, such as dust or broken glass, getting into food while it is being stored or during the preparation processes.

The controls which are put into place must be effective. They must eradicate the risk of harm, or at least reduce it to an acceptable level. From time to time a risk may appear to be so great that it is not practicable to eliminate it without unreasonable expense. In such a case it may be sensible to seek advice on whether the proposed operation can be changed so that the hazard is eliminated. Environmental health officers are usually prepared to give clubs the benefit of their experience on matters such as this.

Staff Training
Those responsible for running a club should ensure that any controls introduced as a result of the risk assessment are properly explained to the staff employed in the preparation or service of food. To be effective, safeguards relating to food and stock rotation, separation of different foodstuffs to avoid cross-contamination, and cooking or reheating food, all need to be fully understood and implemented. The training of staff is clearly important in relation to food hygiene. Courses on the subject are available, and usually lead to certificates of competence. Where in-house training would be difficult, staff should be encouraged to attend an outside course. Again, the local authority is often able to provide information about such courses.

Review of Systems and Processes
Once safe systems are in place, an officer or nominated member of the club should be allocated responsibility for keeping them under frequent review, so that the club can be sure that any food it supplies is safe for human consumption. If the way in which food is received, prepared or supplied to members changes, it may be necessary to

review the systems in place.

Further Information

A succinct guide to the regulations has been published by Eaton Publications, Eaton House, PO Box 34, Walton-on-Thames, Surrey KT12 1LN; telephone: 01932 229 001.

The Department of Health publishes helpful leaflets. They include *Assured Safe Catering*, *A Guide to the General Food Hygiene Regulations* and *A Guide to Food Hazards and your Business*. They are written in straightforward language. Copies can be obtained from The Department of Health, PO Box 410, Wetherby, LS23 7LN.

8. Product Substitution

Some people are not particular about brand when they order a drink. A member or guest may simply order a double scotch without expressing any preference as to the label. In such circumstances, the club is free to supply any brand of scotch it has available. But if the purchaser asks for a specific brand of any product, that brand must be supplied if at all possible. If the requested brand is not available, the bar staff should say so, and offer an alternative, which the member or guest would be free to accept or reject.

Great care is necessary to supply the correct drink. Supplying one brand when another has been ordered without telling the customer is known as "passing off". Trading standards officers take an interest in such occurrences and may visit the premises to obtain evidence. If satisfied that an offence has occurred, charges may be brought.

It is an offence to apply a false trade description to any product sold or offered for sale. The Trade Descriptions Act 1968 provides that "any person who in the course of a trade or business applies a false trade description to any goods, or supplies or offers to supply any goods to which a false trade description is applied, is guilty of an offence".

The maximum penalty for a person convicted in the magistrates' court is a fine not exceeding £5,000; if convicted in a Crown Court, the maximum penalty is an unlimited fine, or imprisonment for a term not exceeding two years, or both.

For the purposes of the Act, "person" includes any body whether it is incorporated or unincorporated; it therefore includes a members' club.

The test of whether a trade description is false is whether an ordinary man would be likely to be misled by it. See the cases of *Concentrated Foods Ltd v Champ* and *Amos v Britvic Ltd*.

This Act also offers a defendant the opportunity to plead a statutory defence. Thus, it is a defence if the defendant proves (on the balance of probabilities):

- that the commission of the offence was due to a mistake, or to reliance on information supplied to the defendant, or to an act or default of another person, or some accident beyond the defendant's control; and
- that the defendant took all reasonable precautions and exercised all due diligence to avoid the commission of the offence by the defendant or any person under the defendant's control.

Again, prior notice of the intention to plead this defence must be given to the prosecution, together with whatever information the defendant has about the identification of any other person whose act or default gave rise to the offence.

Where the offence charged is one of supplying or offering to supply goods to which a false trade description is applied, it is a defence to prove that the defendant did not know, and could not with reasonable diligence have ascertained, that the goods did not conform to the description applied to them.

If there is any evidence that an inexpensive product has been dispensed from a vessel bearing the name of a more expensive brand, and that the payment demanded was appropriate only to the more expensive product, the offender may be charged with obtaining a pecuniary advantage by deception, or with some other offence under the Theft Act 1968.

In addition to a club's duty to its members and guests to ensure they are provided with the brands requested and not with substitutes, it also has a duty to producers not to become involved with "passing off". Understandably, the producers of branded drinks are proud of their products and go to great lengths to see that other brews are not sold in the guise of their own. If they find that their products are being "impersonated", they will almost certainly be prepared to go to the civil courts to obtain an injunction and an order for damages.

9. Prescribed Measures

Clubs are also under a duty to ensure that the drinks they supply conform to the measures prescribed. In particular, spirits may be supplied only in quantities of 25 millilitres or 35 millilitres, or in multiples of those measures; thus, a single measure must be either 25 or 35 millilitres and a double must be either 50 or 70 millilitres. (Weights and Measures (Intoxicating Liquor) Order 1988, Statutory Instrument 1988 No. 2039.)

Those responsible for running club bars should take care that this particular piece of legislation is adhered to. They should also be careful to see it that the measures adopted are the same in all the club's bars. The 1988 Order makes clear that a club cannot have different measures in different bars.

It is in a club's interests that the measures adopted comply with the law, and that members and guests are fully informed of the measures that have been chosen in their club. The best way is to place notices near the bars, setting out the measures being used, along with the tariff.

Chapter 17

Frequently Asked Questions

1. Introduction

Those who manage clubs are sometimes concerned by questions which are not answered in any of the legislation. In such cases, since it is not possible to point to any statutory provision or any case law, it may be difficult to offer definitive guidance. Some of these questions are addressed in this chapter, and advice, based on experience, is offered, in the hope that it will enable clubs to find solutions acceptable to their members. It is recognised that others may give different, although equally sound, advice.

2. Contracting Out Bar Services

Occasionally, because of staffing difficulties or problems with the profitability of its bar, a club may consider contracting out its bar services to a specialist catering organisation. The idea would seem to be that the contractor would then assume responsibility for maintaining profitability and providing adequate staff, while the club continues to receive a profit from its bar.

The author's opinion is that clubs should think long and hard before entering into such an arrangement. The club must continue to meet the legislative requirements which qualify it for the benefits of a club premises certificate. The contracting-out procedure could place constraints on the club's freedom to purchase intoxicating liquor and give rise to a situation in which persons – the contractor and the contractor's staff – receive payment for the purchase and supply of such liquor. This would breach the provisions of the Licensing Act on the purchase and supply of alcohol (see page 101) and would give rise to the question whether the club continues to be established and conducted in good faith and so qualified to hold its club premises certificate.

3. The Storage and Use of Glasses

Surprisingly, perhaps, questions about the use of glasses in club bars. arise often. The include such questions as:

- should glasses be stored upside down?
- should every drink be served in a fresh glass?
- should drinks be served in unbreakable glasses?

The first two questions arise from food hygiene considerations and the third relates to public safety and the maintenance of order. In the first case, the concern is that dust or other debris could get into glasses that are stored rim uppermost, which might then contaminate any drink served in them. In the second case the worry is that a drink might be served in a glass that somebody else has already drunk from.

Food hygiene regulations do not contain specific requirements that glasses should be stored upside down when not in use or that a clean glass should be used every time a drink is supplied. A member or guest supplied with a drink in club premises is entitled to expect that it will be served in a clean glass, but there would seem to be no problem in serving a person with a second drink in the same glass that the first was supplied in, if the drinks are the same, and it is clear that the second drink is to be consumed by the person who drank the first. If there is further concern, advice may be sought from an environmental health officer.

There are no regulations requiring a club to use unbreakable glasses. When dealing with an application for a club premises certificate, however, a licensing authority might be satisfied that it is necessary to impose such a requirement as a condition of the certificate. It has power to do so only if it concludes that such a step is necessary to promote one of the licensing objectives described on page 3. The most likely objective would be the public safety objective, although the prevention of crime and disorder could also be relevant. Such a condition seems more likely to be imposed on a premises licence, but if there is evidence of disorder in a club's premises, which has resulted in injury inflicted by a glass that had been smashed, then the condition could be imposed on a club.

The fact that a club has adopted a policy of using unbreakable glasses should be included in an application for a club premises certificate as one of the steps taken by the club in the interests of promoting the objective of preventing crime and disorder.

4. Drinking-up Time

Since the whole of the Licensing Act 1964 is repealed upon the coming into full force of the Licensing Act 2003, the provisions in relation to drinking-up time then no longer apply. The 2003 Act makes no similar provision because the legislation does not prescribe "permitted hours". Consequently, there was no need to provide for exceptions.

It is likely that the authorities will conclude that it is reasonable for persons who have been supplied with drinks while the club is carrying on the qualifying activity of supplying alcohol to be allowed to consume them. To avoid difficulties, a club might specifically include a drinking-up period in the club operating schedule submitted as part of its application for a club premises certificate.

Clubs must indicate the hours during which the premises are open to members and guests, as well as the hours during which licensable activities take place. While the sale or supply of alcohol is a licensable activity, the *consumption* of alcohol is not. Consequently, if the hours during which the club is open to members and guests extend beyond the time at which sales or supplies of alcohol end, there will be a period during which drinks purchased before the bar closed can be consumed.

5. Doorkeepers

Many magisterial licensing committees adopted a policy of requiring qualified doorkeepers as a condition of a special hours order. Under the Licensing Act 2003, licensing authorities may impose a condition on a club premises certificates that staff must be employed to carry out security activities. Such a condition may be imposed only if the authority is satisfied that it is a necessary step to take in support of a licensing objective. Where such a condition is imposed, there must also be a condition that the security staff employed must be licensed by the Security Industry Authority. This is a requirement of the Private Security Industry Act of 2001.

A licensing authority is also able to impose a condition

providing for the employment of stewards and other persons who do not carry out security activities, again only if such a step is necessary in support of a licensing objective. These individuals need not be registered with the Security Industry Authority.

In the Guidance issued under section 182 of the Licensing Act 2003, the Secretary of State for Culture Media and Sport reiterates that when it is a condition of a club premises certificate that persons must be present at the premises to carry out security activities, for example, as door supervisors, they must be licensed by the Security Industry Authority (paragraph 7.70). It goes on to point out that such registration may not be necessary in the case of other individuals, such as stewards employed to provide advice and to ensure the safety of persons visiting the premises, and underlines the need for clarity when conditions are formulated (paragraph 7.71).

6. Staff Becoming Club Members

There is nothing in legislation or case law to prevent a member of staff from becoming a member of the club, or *vice versa*. If the members of the club do not wish staff to be eligible for membership, they can include such a prohibition in the rules of the club. The club would be bound to adhere to such a rule.

A member of staff who is also a member of the club must, as a general rule, be allowed to attend general meetings of the club, to vote, and to be voted into office or onto the club management committee(s). There may, of course, be circumstances in which it would not be appropriate for a member of staff who is also a club member to attend a meeting or to vote. If, for example, the staff member's situation at the club is scheduled for discussion, that discussion might be less inhibited if the staff member were not present all the time. The staff member's point of view must be considered. The person should be allowed to address the meeting or submit views in writing, but should not vote on the issue. It would be good practice for the basis of any decision reached to be communicated to the person affected. If the person is allowed to be present, he or she should certainly declare an interest when the item in question is about to be discussed.

7.   Ending an Affiliation

The special relationship that may exist between a club and a parent body has been mentioned elsewhere. The club may be bound to a considerable extent by the rules of the parent organisation and may be able to make amendments only with its consent. Benefits usually ensue from such an affiliation but the possibility of ending it may arise. For example, if the aims and objects of the club have changed to the point that they are far removed from those of the parent organisation, it may no longer be sensible for the affiliation to continue. Generally, if a club wishes to become independent it would need to dissolve and form a new club. A club can be dissolved only with the agreement of the majority of members. As a result, some work may need to be done to convince the majority that the process of dissolution and reconstitution is worthwhile.

One aspect of such a change which should be considered carefully is that the existing club has "grandfather rights" under the Licensing Act 2003, that is, the conversion of its old club registration certificate into a new club premises certificate is virtually automatic. A new club would have to apply afresh.

8.   Disposal of Property Following Dissolution

As explained in Chapter 1, the premises and other assets of a members' club belong to the members collectively and, as a general rule, in equal shares. There are exceptions to the general rule. For example, the premises used by a club for qualifying activities may be owned by a company, as where the club is primarily for company employees, or by some other independent landlord. In the case of clubs which are limited companies, members may be shareholders in unequal proportions and so entitled to varying shares in the assets on dissolution.

Where the general rule applies, if the members vote for the dissolution of the club, the premises and other assets should be capitalised and distributed among the persons who were paid-up members at the date of dissolution. People who have ceased to be members before the decision to dissolve the club was taken are not entitled to a share of the capitalised assets, even though they may have been members of the club for many years. If the club is a corporation, shareholders will have an interest in the assets even though they have ceased to be members.

137

Appendix A

Forms

[Insert name and address of relevant licensing authority and its reference number (optional)]

(Part A) Application for an Existing Club Certificate to be Converted to a Club Premises Certificate under the Licensing Act 2003 and (Part B) Application to Vary the Club Premises Certificate Simultaneously

PLEASE READ THE FOLLOWING INSTRUCTIONS FIRST

Before completing this form please read the guidance notes at the end of the form. If you are completing this form by hand please write legibly in block capitals. In all cases ensure that your answers are inside the boxes and written in black ink. Use additional sheets if necessary.

You may wish to keep a copy of the completed form for your records.

We [insert name of club] apply to convert an existing club certificate to a club premises certificate under Schedule 8 to the Licensing Act 2003 for the club premises described in Part A1 below

Part A1 – Premises Details

Postal address of club premises or, if none, ordnance survey map reference or description_____

Post town _____Post code_____

Name of person performing duties of a secretary to the club_____

Address of person performing duties of a secretary to the club_____

Post town _____Post code_____

Daytime contact telephone number (if any)_____

E-mail address (optional)_____

Telephone number of premises (if any) _____

Non-domestic rateable value of club premises: £_____

Part A2 – Club Operating Schedule

Where 5,000 or more people attend the club premises at the same time, please state the number_____

General description of club premises (please read guidance note 1)___

_____

What existing qualifying club activities are authorised by your existing club certificate(s)?   Please tick √ Yes

Provision of entertainment

a) plays   ☐
b) films   ☐
c) indoor sporting events   ☐
d) boxing or wrestling entertainment   ☐
e) live music   ☐
f) recorded music   ☐
g) a performance of dance   ☐
h) anything of a similar description to that falling within
    (e), (f) or (g)   ☐

Provision of entertainment facilities for:

i) making music ☐

j) dancing ☐

k) entertainment of a similar description to that falling within
(i) or (j) ☐

Supply of alcohol for members and guests

a) for consumption on the premises ☐

b) for consumption off the premises ☐

State any limitations on the hours during which you are permitted by your certificate(s) or any additional authorisations to conduct club qualifying activities, including the supply of alcohol_____

_____

Describe the conditions subject to which your existing certificate(s) has/ have been granted (please read guidance note 2):

a) General – all four licensing objectives (b,c,d,e)_____

b) The prevention of crime and disorder_____

c) Public safety_____

d) The prevention of public nuisance _____

e) The protection of children from harm_____

Please tick √ Yes

- I have made or enclosed payment of the fee ☐
- I have enclosed the existing certificate(s) or a certified copy of each certificate ☐
- I have enclosed a plan of the club premises ☐
- I have enclosed a copy of the club rules ☐
- I have sent copies of this application to the chief officer of police (please read guidance note 3) ☐
- I understand that if I do not comply with the above requirements my application will be rejected ☐

IT IS AN OFFENCE, LIABLE ON CONVICTION TO A FINE UP TO LEVEL 5 ON THE STANDARD SCALE, UNDER SECTION 158 OF THE LICENSING ACT 2003 TO MAKE A FALSE STATEMENT IN OR IN CONNECTION WITH THIS APPLICATION

Part A3 – Signatures (please read guidance note 4)

Signature for and on behalf of [insert name of club]. (Please read guidance note 5)

Signature_____

Date_____ Capacity_____

Contact name (where not previously given) and address for correspondence associated with this application (please read guidance note 16) _____

Post town_____Post code_____

IF YOU WISH TO APPLY SIMULTANEOUSLY FOR A VARIATION OF THE CLUB
PREMISES CERTIFICATE IF IT IS CONVERTED FROM YOUR EXISTING CLUB
CERTIFICATE(S) UNDER SECTION 84 OF THE LICENSING ACT 2003, NOW
COMPLETE PART B OF THIS FORM.
IF YOU DO NOT WISH TO APPLY SIMULTANEOUSLY FOR A VARIATION OF
THE CLUB PREMISES CERTIFICATE IF IT IS CONVERTED FROM YOUR
EXISTING CLUB CERTIFICATE(S), YOU SHOULD LEAVE PART B BLANK.

PART B - Application to vary a club premises certificate under the Licensing Act 2003

[Insert name of club] being the proposed club premises certificate holder of
an existing club certificate to be converted under the terms of Schedule 8
to the Licensing Act 2003 apply to vary it under section 84 of the Licensing
Act 2003 for the premises described in Part A above.

Part B1 - Variation

Please tick √

Do you want the proposed variation to have effect from the
second appointed day? ☐

If not, when do you want the variation to take effect from [Day Month Year]

If your proposed variation would mean that 5,000 or more people are
expected to attend the club premises at the same time, please state the
number expected to attend_____

Please describe briefly the nature of the proposed variation (please read
guidance note 1)_____

Part B2 – Club Operating Schedule

Please complete those parts of the club operating schedule which would
be subject to change if this application to vary were successful.

What club qualifying activities do you now intend to conduct on the club
premises and/or at what varied times do you intend to conduct them?
(please see section 1 of the Licensing Act 2003 and Schedule 1 to the
Licensing Act 2003)

Please tick √ Yes

Provision of regulated entertainment
a) plays (if ticking yes, fill in box A) ☐
b) films (if ticking yes, fill in box B) ☐
c) indoor sporting events (if ticking yes, fill in box C) ☐
d) boxing or wrestling entertainment (if ticking yes, fill in box D) ☐
e) live music (if ticking yes, fill in box E) ☐
f) recorded music (if ticking yes, fill in box F) ☐
g) performances of dance (if ticking yes, fill in box G) ☐
h) anything of a similar description to that falling within
(e), (f) or (g) (if ticking yes, fill in box H) ☐

Provision of entertainment facilities:
i) making music (if ticking yes, fill in box I) ☐

j) dancing (if ticking yes, fill in box J) ☐
k) entertainment of a similar description to that falling within
(j) or (k) (if ticking yes, fill in box K) ☐

Supply of alcohol (if ticking yes, fill in box L) ☐
a) the supply of alcohol by or on behalf of a club to, or to the
order of, a member of the club ☐
b) the sale by retail of alcohol by or on behalf of a club to a
guest of a member of the club for consumption on the
premises where the sale takes place ☐

IN ALL CASES COMPLETE BOXES M, N and O.

A
Plays
Standard days and timings
(please read guidance note 6)

Day	Start	Finish
Mon	_____	_____
Tue	_____	_____
Wed	_____	_____
Thur	_____	_____
Fri	_____	_____
Sat	_____	_____
Sun	_____	_____

Will the performance of a play take place indoors or outdoors or both - please tick √ (please read guidance note 7)
Indoors ☐
Outdoors ☐
Both ☐

Please give further details here (please read guidance note 8)_____

State any seasonal variations for performing plays (please read guidance note 9)_____

Non standard timings. Where you intend to use the premises for the performance of plays at different times to those listed in the column on the left, please list (please read guidance note 10)_____

B
Films
Standard days and timings
(please read guidance note 6)

Day	Start	Finish
Mon	_____	_____
Tue	_____	_____
Wed	_____	_____
Thur	_____	_____
Fri	_____	_____
Sat	_____	_____
Sun	_____	_____

Will the exhibition of films take place indoors or outdoors or both - please tick √ (please read guidance note 7)
Indoors ☐
Outdoors ☐
Both ☐

Please give further details here (please read guidance note 8)_____

State any seasonal variations for the exhibition of films (please read guidance note 9)_____

Non standard timings. Where you intend to use the premises for the exhibition of films at different times to those listed in the column on the left, please list (please read guidance note 10)_____

C
Indoor sporting events
Standard days and timings
(please read guidance note 6)

Day	Start	Finish
Mon	_____	_____
Tue	_____	_____
Wed	_____	_____
Thur	_____	_____
Fri	_____	_____
Sat	_____	_____
Sun	_____	_____

Please give further details (please read guidance note 8)_____

State any seasonal variations for indoor sporting events (please read guidance note 9)

Non standard timings. Where you intend to use the premises for indoor sporting events at different times to those listed in the column on the left, please list (please read guidance note 10)_____

143

D
Boxing or wrestling entertainment

Standard days and timings
(please read guidance note 6)

Day	Start	Finish
Mon	_____	_____
Tue	_____	_____
Wed	_____	_____
Thur	_____	_____
Fri	_____	_____
Sat	_____	_____
Sun	_____	_____

Will the boxing or wrestling entertainment take place indoors or outdoors or both - please tick √
(please read guidance note 7)

Indoors ☐
Outdoors ☐
Both ☐

Please give further details here (please read guidance note 8)_____

State any seasonal variations for boxing or wrestling entertainment (please read guidance note 9)_____

Non standard timings. Where you intend to use the premises for boxing or wrestling entertainment at different times to those listed in the column on the left, please list (please read guidance note 10)_____

E
Live music

Standard timings
(please read guidance note 6)

Day	Start	Finish
Mon	_____	_____
Tue	_____	_____
Wed	_____	_____
Thur	_____	_____
Fri	_____	_____
Sat	_____	_____
Sun	_____	_____

Will the performance of live music take place indoors or outdoors or both - please tick √
(please read guidance note 7)

Indoors ☐
Outdoors ☐
Both ☐

Please give further details here (please read guidance note 8)_____

State any seasonal variations for the performance of live music (please read guidance note 9)_____

Non standard timings. Where you intend to use the premises for the performance of live music at different times to those listed in the column on the left, please list (please read guidance note 10)_____

F
Recorded music

Standard days and timings
(please read guidance note 6)

Day	Start	Finish
Mon	_____	_____
Tue	_____	_____
Wed	_____	_____
Thur	_____	_____
Fri	_____	_____
Sat	_____	_____
Sun	_____	_____

Will the playing of recorded music take place indoors or outdoors or both - please tick √
(please read guidance note 7)

Indoors ☐
Outdoors ☐
Both ☐

Please give further details here (please read guidance note 8)_____

State any seasonal variations for playing recorded music (please read guidance note 9)_____

Non standard timings. Where you intend to use the premises for the playing of recorded music at different times to those listed in the column on the left, please list (please read guidance note 10)_____

G
Performance of dance

Standard days and timings
(please read guidance note 6)

Day	Start	Finish
Mon	_____	_____
Tue	_____	_____
Wed	_____	_____
Thur	_____	_____
Fri	_____	_____

Will the performance of dance take place indoors or outdoors or both - please tick √
(please read guidance note 7)

Indoors ☐
Outdoors ☐
Both ☐

Please give further details here (please read guidance note 8)_____

State any seasonal variations for the performance of dance (please read guidance note 9)_____

Sat _____ _____
Sun _____ _____

Non standard timings. Where you intend to use the premises for the performance of dance entertainment at different times to those listed in the column on the left, please list (please read guidance note 10)_____

H
Anything of a similar description to that falling within (e), (f) or (g)
Standard days and timings
(please read guidance note 6)

Day	Start	Finish
Mon	_____	_____
Tue	_____	_____
Wed	_____	_____
Thur	_____	_____
Fri	_____	_____
Sat	_____	_____
Sun	_____	_____

Please give a description of the type of entertainment you will be providing_____

Will this entertainment take place indoors or outdoors or both - please tick √ (please read guidance note 7)	Indoors	☐
	Outdoors	☐
	Both	☐

Please give further details here (please read guidance note 8)_____

State any seasonal variations for entertainment of a similar description to that falling within (e), (f) or (g) (please read guidance note 9)_____

Non standard timings. Where you intend to use the premises for the entertainment of similar description to that falling within (e), (f) or (g) at different times to those listed in the column on the left, please list (please read guidance note 10)_____

I
Provision of facilities for making music
Standard days and timings
(please read guidance note 6)

Day	Start	Finish
Mon	_____	_____
Tue	_____	_____
Wed	_____	_____
Thur	_____	_____
Fri	_____	_____
Sat	_____	_____
Sun	_____	_____

Please give a description of the facilities for making music you will be providing_____

Will the facilities for making music be indoors or outdoors or both - please tick √ (please read guidance note 7)	Indoors	☐
	Outdoors	☐
	Both	☐

Please give further details here (please read guidance note 8)_____

State any seasonal variations for the provision of facilities for making music (please read guidance note 9)_____

Non standard timings. Where you intend to use the premises for provision of facilities for making music entertainment at different times to those listed in the column on the left, please list (please read guidance note 10)_____

J
Provision of facilities for dancing
Standard days and timings
(please read guidance note 6)

Day	Start	Finish
Mon	_____	_____
Tue	_____	_____
Wed	_____	_____
Thur	_____	_____
Fri	_____	_____
Sat	_____	_____
Sun	_____	_____

Will the facilities for dancing be indoors or outdoors or both – please tick √ (please read guidance note 7)	Indoors	☐
	Outdoors	☐
	Both	☐

Please give further details here (please read guidance note 8)_____

State any seasonal variations for providing dancing facilities (please read guidance note 9)_____

Non standard timings. Where you intend to use the premises for the provision of facilities for dancing entertainment at different times to those listed in the column on the left, please list (please read guidance note 10)_____

145

K
Provision of facilities for entertainment of a similar description to that falling within I or J

Please give a description of the type of entertainment facility you will be providing_____
_____
_____

Standard days and timings (please read guidance note 6)

Day	Start	Finish
Mon	_____	_____
Tue	_____	_____
Wed	_____	_____
Thur	_____	_____
Fri	_____	_____
Sat	_____	_____
Sun	_____	_____

Will the entertainment facility be indoors or outdoors or both – please tick √ (please read guidance note 7)

Indoors ☐
Outdoors ☐
Both ☐

Please give further details here (please read guidance note 8)_____
_____

State any seasonal variations for the provision of facilities for entertainment of a similar description to that falling within I or J (please read guidance note 9)_____

Non standard timings. Where you intend to use the premises for the provision of facilities for entertainment of a similar description to that falling within I or J at different times to those listed in the column on the left, please list (please read guidance note 10)_____

L
Supply of alcohol

Standard days and timings (please read guidance note 6)

Day	Start	Finish
Mon	_____	_____
Tue	_____	_____
Wed	_____	_____
Thur	_____	_____
Fri	_____	_____
Sat	_____	_____
Sun	_____	_____

Will the supply of alcohol be for for consumption: - please tick √ box (please read guidance note 11)

On the premises ☐
Off the premises ☐
Both ☐

State any proposed seasonal variations for the supply of alcohol (please read guidance note 9)_____
_____

Non standard timings. Where you intend to use the premises for the supply of alcohol at different times to those listed in the column on the left, please list (please read guidance note 10)_____
_____

M
Please highlight any adult entertainment or services, activities, other entertainment or matters ancillary to the use of the club premises that may give rise to concern in respect of children (please read guidance note 12)

N
Please identify any of the conditions, terms or restrictions currently imposed on the converted certificate which the club believes could be removed as a consequence of the proposed variation it is seeking

O
Please describe any additional steps that you intend to take in order to promote the four licensing objectives if the proposed variation is granted:
a) General – all four licensing objectives (b,c,d,e) (please read guidance note 13)_____
b) The prevention of crime and disorder_____
c) Public safety_____
d) The prevention of public nuisance_____
e) The protection of children from harm_____

146

Please tick √ Yes

- I have sent copies of this application to vary to
  responsible authorities and others where applicable ☐
- I understand that I must now advertise my application
  to vary ☐
- I understand that if I do not comply with the above
  requirements my application to vary will be rejected ☐

Part B3 – Signatures (please read guidance note 4)
Signature for and on behalf of [insert name of club] (see guidance note 15)
Signature_____

Date_____ Capacity_____

Contact name (where not previously given) and address for
  correspondence associated with this application (please read guidance
  note 16) _____

Post town_____Post code_____

Notes for Guidance
PART A
1. Describe the premises. For example the type of premises, its general situation
   and layout and any other information which could be relevant to the licensing
   objectives. Where your application includes off-supplies of alcohol and you
   intend to provide a place for consumption of these off-supplies you must include
   a description of where the place is and its proximity to the premises.
2. Where the conditions to which your existing certificate(s) is granted do not relate
   solely to any one of the four licensing objectives, please describe such
   conditions in the general box.
3. The law requires you to send a mandatory copy of this application to the chief
   officer of police for that area at the same time as sending to the local licensing
   authority.
4. The application form must be signed.
5. A club's agent (for example solicitor) may sign the form on its behalf provided
   that they have actual authority to do so.

PART B
This application cannot be used to vary the club premises certificate to vary
substantially the premises to which it relates. If you wish to make that type of
change to the club premises certificate you should make a new club premises
certificate application under the Licensing Act 2003.
6. Please give timings in 24 hour clock.
7. Where taking place in a building or other structure, please tick as appropriate.
   Indoors may include a tent.
8. Please state type of activity to be authorised, if not already stated, and give
   relevant further details, for example (but not exclusively) whether or not music
   will be amplified or unamplified.
9. For example (but not exclusively), where the activity will occur on additional
   days during the summer months
10. For example (but not exclusively), where you wish the activity to go on longer on
    a particular day e.g. Christmas Eve.
11. If you wish people to be able to consume alcohol on the premises please tick
    on, if you wish people to be able to purchase alcohol to consume away from the

premises please tick off. If you wish people to be able to do both please tick both.

12. Please give information about anything to occur at the premises or ancillary to the use of the premises which may give rise to concern in respect of children, for example (but not exclusively) nudity or semi-nudity, films for restricted age groups, the presence of gambling machines.

13. Please list here steps you will take to promote all four licensing objectives together.

14. The application form must be signed.

15. A club's agent (for example solicitor) may sign the form on their behalf provided that they have actual authority to do so.

16. This is the address which we shall use to correspond with you about this application.

[Insert name and address of relevant licensing authority and its reference number (optional)]

PART A Declaration for a Club Premises Certificate to be Granted under the Licensing Act 2003

PLEASE READ THE FOLLOWING INSTRUCTIONS BEFORE COMPLETING DECLARATION

Before completing this form please read the guidance notes at the end of the form. If you are completing this form by hand please write legibly in block capitals. In all cases ensure that your answers are inside the boxes and written in black ink. Use additional sheets if necessary.

You may wish to keep a copy of the completed form for your records.

Club Premises Details

Name of club_____

Postal address of club, if any, or, if none, ordnance survey map reference

or description_____

Post town _____Post code_____

Telephone number (if any)_____

E-mail (optional)_____

Club Declaration as to Qualifying Status

[Insert name of club] club makes the following declarations

1) Where the club to which this application relates is:

a registered society within the meaning of the Industrial and Provident Societies Act 1965;

a registered society within the meaning of the Friendly Societies Act 1974; or

a registered friendly society within the meaning of the Friendly Societies Act,

the club declares that the club satisfies:

Please tick √ Yes

Condition 1 in section 62(2) of the Licensing Act 2003   ☐
Please give relevant club rule number(s) _____

Condition 2 in section 62(3) of the Licensing Act 2003   ☐
Please give relevant club rule number(s)_____

Condition 4 in section 62(5) of the Licensing Act 2003_____   ☐

Does the club wish to supply alcohol to members and guests? ☐
If yes the club declares that–
The purchase of alcohol for the club and the supply of alcohol
by the club is under the control of the members or of a   ☐
committee appointed by the members
Please give relevant club rule number(s), if any_____

2) Where the club to which this application relates is:

an association organised for the social well-being and recreation of persons employed in or about coal mines, the club declares that the club satisfies:

Please tick √ Yes

Condition 1 in section 62(2) of the Licensing Act 2003 ☐
Please give relevant club rule number(s)_____

Condition 2 in section 62(3) of the Licensing Act 2003 ☐
Please give relevant club rule number(s)_____

Does the club wish to supply alcohol to members and
    guests? ☐
If yes the club declares that it satisfies–

First condition in section 66(4) of the Licensing Act 2003 ☐
Please give relevant club rule number(s), if any_____

Second condition in section 66(5) of the Licensing Act 2003 ☐
Please give relevant club rule number(s), if any_____

3) Where the club to which this application relates does not fall into the
    categories in 1 or 2 above, the club declares that the club satisfies:

Please tick √ Yes

Condition 1 in section 62(2) of the Licensing Act 2003 ☐
Please give relevant club rule number(s)_____

Condition 2 in section 62(3) of the Licensing Act 2003 ☐
Please give relevant club rule number(s)_____

Condition 3 in section 62(4) of the Licensing Act 2003 ☐

The club's arrangements for restricting the club's freedom of purchase of
    alcohol are:
(a) contained in club rule number(s)_____
(b) or, as follows (*Please provide a short description*)_____
_____

The club's provisions by which money or property of the club or any gain
arising from the carrying on of the club is or may be applied for charitable
benevolent or political purposes are:
(a) contained in club rule number(s) _____
(b) or, as follows (*Please provide a short description*)_____
_____

The arrangements for giving members information about the finances of
the club are:
(a) contained in club rule number(s), _____
(b) or, as follows (*Please provide a short description*)_____
_____

Please describe details of the books of account and other records kept to
    ensure the accuracy of the information about finances given to
    members of the club or give the relevant rule number(s)_____
_____

Please tick √ Yes

Condition 4 in section 62(5) of the Licensing Act 2003 ☐

Condition 5 in section 62(6) of the Licensing Act 2003 ☐

The club proposes to supply alcohol to members and guests
and declares that the club satisfies:

additional condition 1 in section 64(2) of the Licensing Act 2003 ☐
Please give relevant club rule number(s), if any_____

additional condition 2 in section 64(3) of the Licensing Act 2003 ☐
Please give relevant rule number(s), if any_____

additional condition 3 in section 64(4) of the Licensing Act 2003 ☐
Please give relevant club rule number(s), if any_____

IT IS AN OFFENCE, LIABLE ON CONVICTION TO A FINE UP TO LEVEL 5 ON
THE STANDARD SCALE, UNDER SECTION 158 OF THE LICENSING ACT 2003
TO MAKE A FALSE STATEMENT IN OR IN CONNECTION WITH THIS
APPLICATION

I, _____, make this declaration on behalf of the club and have
authority to bind the club
Signature _____Date _____Capacity_____

Part B: Application for a Club Premises Certificate to be Granted under the Licensing Act 2003
PLEASE READ THE FOLLOWING INSTRUCTIONS BEFORE COMPLETING APPLICATION

Before completing this form please read the guidance notes at the end of the form
If you are completing this form by hand please write legibly in block capitals. In all
cases ensure that your answers are inside the boxes and written in black ink. Use
additional sheets if necessary.
You may wish to keep a copy of the completed form for your records.

(Insert name of club) club applies for a club premises certificate under
section 71 of the Licensing Act 2003 for the premises described in Part 1
below (the club premises)

The club is making this application to you as the relevant licensing
authority in accordance with section 68 of the Licensing Act 2003

Part 1 – Club premises details
Name of club_____
Postal address of premises or, if none, ordnance survey map reference or
description_____
Post town _____Post code_____
Telephone number (if any)_____
E-mail address (optional)_____
Name of person performing duties of a secretary to the club_____
Address of person performing duties of a secretary to the club_____
Post town _____Post code_____
Daytime contact telephone number (if any)_____
E-mail address (optional)_____
Non-domestic rateable value of club premises: £_____

Are the club premises occupied and habitually used by the
club   Yes ☐   No ☐

Part 2 – Club Operating Schedule

When do you want the club premises certificate to
start?   [Day Month Year]
If you wish the certificate to be valid only for a limited period,
when do you want it to end?   [Day Month Year]

If 5,000 or more people are expected to attend the premises at any one
time, please state the number expected to attend_____

General description of club (please read guidance note 1)_____

_____

What qualifying club activities do you intend to conduct on the club
premises?_____

Provision of entertainment   Please tick √ Yes
a) plays (if ticking yes, fill in box A)   ☐
b) films (if ticking yes, fill in box B)   ☐
c) indoor sporting events (if ticking yes, fill in box C)   ☐
d) boxing or wrestling entertainment (if ticking yes, fill in box D)☐
e) live music (if ticking yes, fill in box E)   ☐
f) recorded music (if ticking yes, fill in box F)   ☐
g) performance of dance (if ticking yes, fill in box G)   ☐
h) anything of a similar description to that falling within
    (e), (f) or (g) (if ticking yes, fill in box H)   ☐

Provision of entertainment facilities for:
i) making music (if ticking yes, fill in box I)   ☐
j) dancing (if ticking yes, fill in box J)   ☐
k) entertainment of a similar description to that falling within
    (i) or (j) (if ticking yes, fill in box K)   ☐

**The supply of alcohol by or on behalf of a club to, or to the order of, a
member of the club** (if ticking yes, fill in box L)   ☐

**The sale by retail of alcohol by or on behalf of a club to a guest of a
member of the club for consumption on the premises where the
sale takes place** (if ticking yes, fill in box L)   ☐

In all cases complete boxes M, N, and O

A
Plays

Standard days and timings (please read guidance note 6)	Will the performance of a play take place indoors or outdoors or both - please tick √ (please read guidance note 2)

Indoors ☐ Outdoors ☐ Both ☐

Day Start Finish
Mon _____ _____
Tue _____ _____   Please give further details here (please read guidance
Wed _____ _____   note 3)_____
Thur _____ _____   _____
Fri _____ _____   State any seasonal variations for performing plays (please
Sat _____ _____   read guidance note 4)_____
Sun _____ _____   _____
                       Non standard timings. Where the club intends to use the

premises for the performance of plays at different times from those listed in the column on the left, please list (please read guidance note 5)_____

B
Films
Standard days and timings
(please read guidance note 6)

Day	Start	Finish
Mon	_____	_____
Tue	_____	_____
Wed	_____	_____
Thur	_____	_____
Fri	_____	_____
Sat	_____	_____
Sun	_____	_____

Will the exhibition of films take place indoors or outdoors or both - please tick √
(please read guidance note 2)

Indoors ☐
Outdoors ☐
Both ☐

Please give further details here (please read guidance note 3)_____

State any seasonal variations for the exhibition of films (please read guidance note 4)_____

Non standard timings. Where the club intends to use the premises for the exhibition of film at different times from those listed in the column on the left, please list (please read guidance note 5)_____

C
Indoor sporting events
Standard days and timings
(please read guidance note 6)

Day	Start	Finish
Mon	_____	_____
Tue	_____	_____
Wed	_____	_____
Thur	_____	_____
Fri	_____	_____
Sat	_____	_____
Sun	_____	_____

Please give further details here (please read guidance note 3)_____

State any seasonal variations for indoor sporting events (please read guidance note 4)_____

Non standard timings. Where the club intends to use the premises for indoor sporting events at different times from those listed in the column on the left, please list (please read guidance note 5)_____

D
Boxing or wrestling entertainments
Standard days and timings
(please read guidance note 6)

Day	Start	Finish
Mon	_____	_____
Tue	_____	_____
Wed	_____	_____
Thur	_____	_____
Fri	_____	_____
Sat	_____	_____
Sun	_____	_____

Will the boxing or wrestling entertainment take place indoors or outdoors or both - please tick √
(please read guidance note 2)

Indoors ☐
Outdoors ☐
Both ☐

Please give further details here (please read guidance note 3)_____

State any seasonal variations for boxing or wrestling entertainment (please read guidance note 4)_____

Non standard timings. Where the club intends to use the premises for boxing or wrestling entertainment at different times from those listed in the column on the left, please list (please read guidance note 5)_____

E
Live music
Standard timings
(please read guidance note 6)

Day	Start	Finish
Mon	_____	_____
Tue	_____	_____
Wed	_____	_____
Thur	_____	_____
Fri	_____	_____

Will the performance of live music take place indoors or outdoors or both - please tick √
(please read guidance note 2)

Indoors ☐
Outdoors ☐
Both ☐

Please give further details here (please read guidance note 3)_____

State any seasonal variations for the performance of live music (please read guidance note 4)_____

Sat _____ _____
Sun _____ _____

Non standard timings. Where the club intends to use the premises for the performance of live music at different times from those listed in the column on the left, please list (please read guidance note 5)_____

F
Recorded music

Standard days and timings
(please read guidance note 6)

Day	Start	Finish
Mon	_____	_____
Tue	_____	_____
Wed	_____	_____
Thur	_____	_____
Fri	_____	_____
Sat	_____	_____
Sun	_____	_____

Will the playing of recorded music take place indoors or outdoors or both - please tick √ (please read guidance note 2)

Indoors	☐
Outdoors	☐
Both	☐

Please give further details here (please read guidance note 3)_____

State any seasonal variations for playing recorded music (please read guidance note 4)_____

Non standard timings. Where the club intends to use the premises for the playing of recorded music at different times from those listed in the column on the left, please list (please read guidance note 5)_____

G
Performance of dance

Standard days and timings
(please read guidance note 6)

Day	Start	Finish
Mon	_____	_____
Tue	_____	_____
Wed	_____	_____
Thur	_____	_____
Fri	_____	_____
Sat	_____	_____
Sun	_____	_____

Will the performance of dance take place indoors or outdoors or both - please tick √ (please read guidance note 2)

Indoors	☐
Outdoors	☐
Both	☐

Please give further details here (please read guidance note 3)_____

State any seasonal variations for the performance of dance (please read guidance note 4)_____

Non standard timings. Where the club intends to use the premises for the performance of dance at different times from those listed in the column on the left, please list (please read guidance note 5)_____

H
Anything of a similar description to that falling within (e), (f) or (g)

Standard days and timings
(please read guidance note 6)

Day	Start	Finish
Mon	_____	_____
Tue	_____	_____
Wed	_____	_____
Thur	_____	_____
Fri	_____	_____
Sat	_____	_____
Sun	_____	_____

Please give a description of the type of entertainment that the club will be providing_____

Will this entertainment take place indoors or outdoors or both - please tick √ (please read guidance note 2)

Indoors	☐
Outdoors	☐
Both	☐

Please give further details here (please read guidance note 3)_____

State any seasonal variations for entertainment (please read guidance note 4)_____

Non standard timings. Where the club intends to use the premises for the entertainment at different times from those listed in the column on the left, please list (please read guidance note 5)_____

154

I
Provision of facilities for making music

Standard days and timings
(please read guidance note 6)

Day	Start	Finish
Mon	_____	_____
Tue	_____	_____
Wed	_____	_____
Thur	_____	_____
Fri	_____	_____
Sat	_____	_____
Sun	_____	_____

Please give a description of the type of facilities for making music that the club will be providing_____

Will the facilities for making music be indoors or outdoors or both - please tick √ (please read guidance note 2)

Indoors	☐
Outdoors	☐
Both	☐

Please give further details here (please read guidance note 3)_____

State any seasonal variations for the provision of facilities for making music (please read guidance note 4)_____

Non standard timings. Where the club intends to use the premises for the provision of facilities for making music entertainment at different times from those listed in the column on the left, please list (please read guidance note 5)_____

J
Provision of facilities for dancing

Standard days and timings
(please read guidance note 6)

Day	Start	Finish
Mon	_____	_____
Tue	_____	_____
Wed	_____	_____
Thur	_____	_____
Fri	_____	_____
Sat	_____	_____
Sun	_____	_____

Please give a description of the type of facilities for dancing that the club will be providing_____

Will the facilities for dancing be indoors or outdoors or both - please tick √ (please read guidance note 2)

Indoors	☐
Outdoors	☐
Both	☐

Please give further details here (please read guidance note 3)_____

State any seasonal variations for the provision of dancing facilities (please read guidance note 4)_____

Non standard timings. Where the club intends to use the premises for the provision of dancing facilities at different times from those listed in the column on the left, please list (please read guidance note 5)_____

K
Provision of facilities for entertainment of a similar description to that falling within I or J

Standard days and timings
(please read guidance note 6)

Day	Start	Finish
Mon	_____	_____
Tue	_____	_____
Wed	_____	_____
Thur	_____	_____
Fri	_____	_____
Sat	_____	_____
Sun	_____	_____

Please give a description of the type of entertainment facility the club will be providing_____

Will the entertainment facility be indoors or outdoors or both – please tick √ (please read guidance note 2)

Indoors	☐
Outdoors	☐
Both	☐

Please give further details here (please read guidance note 3)_____

State any seasonal variations for the provision of this entertainment facility (please read guidance note 4)_____

Non standard timings. Where the club intends to use the premises for the provision of entertainment facilities at different times from those listed in the column on the left, please list (please read guidance note 5)_____

L
Supply of alcohol
Standard days and timings
(please read guidance note 6)

Day	Start	Finish
Mon	_____	_____
Tue	_____	_____
Wed	_____	_____
Thur	_____	_____
Fri	_____	_____
Sat	_____	_____
Sun	_____	_____

Will the supply of alcohol be for consumption:
- please tick √ box
(please read guidance note 7)

On the premises ☐
Off the premises ☐
Both ☐

State any seasonal variations (please read guidance note 4)_____

Non standard timings. Where the club intends to use the premises for the supply of alcohol at different times from those listed in the column on the left, please list (please read guidance note 5)_____

M
Hours club premises are open to the members and guests
Standard days and timings
(please read guidance note 6)

Day	Start	Finish
Mon	_____	_____
Tue	_____	_____
Wed	_____	_____
Thur	_____	_____
Fri	_____	_____
Sat	_____	_____
Sun	_____	_____

State any seasonal variations (please read guidance note 4)_____

Non standard timings. Where you intend the premises to be open to the members and guests at different times from those listed in the column on the left, please list (please read guidance note 5)_____

N
Please highlight any adult entertainment or services, activities, other entertainment or matters ancillary to the use of the club premises that may give rise to concern in respect of children (please read guidance note 8)

O
Describe the steps you intend to take to promote the four licensing objectives:
a) General – all four licensing objectives (b,c,d,e) (please read guidance note 9)_____
b) The prevention of crime and disorder_____
c) Public safety_____
d) The prevention of public nuisance_____
e) The protection of children from harm_____

Please tick √ Yes
- I have made or enclosed payment of the fee ☐
- I have enclosed the plan of the premises ☐
- I have sent copies of this application and plan to the responsible authorities ☐
- I have completed and enclosed the club declaration and enclose a copy of the club rules ☐
- I understand that I must now advertise my application ☐
- I understand that if I do not comply with the above requirements my application will be rejected ☐

IT IS AN OFFENCE, LIABLE ON CONVICTION TO A FINE OF UP TO LEVEL 5 ON THE STANDARD SCALE UNDER SECTION 158 OF THE LICENSING ACT 2003 TO MAKE A FALSE STATEMENT IN OR IN CONNECTION WITH THIS APPLICATION.

Part 3 – Signatures (please read guidance note 10)

I [Insert full name] make this application on behalf of the club and have authority to bind the club.

Signature_____

Date_____ Capacity_____

Address for correspondence associated with this application (please read guidance note 11) _____

Post town_____Post code_____

Telephone number (if any)_____

If you would prefer us to correspond with you by e-mail your e-mail address (optional)_____

Notes for Guidance

1. Describe the premises. For example the type of premises, its general situation and layout and any other information which could be relevant to the licensing objectives. Where your application includes off-supplies of alcohol and you intend to provide a place for consumption of these off-supplies you must include a description of where the place will be and its proximity to the premises.
2. Where taking place in a building or other structure please tick as appropriate. Indoors may include a tent.
3. Please state type of activity to be authorised, if not already stated, and give relevant further details, for example (but not exclusively) whether or not music will be amplified or unamplified.
4. For example (but not exclusively) where the activity will occur on additional days during the summer months.
5. For example (but not exclusively), where you wish the activity to go on longer on a particular day, e.g. Christmas Eve.
6. Please give timings in 24 hour clock. (eg 16:00) and only give details for the days of the week when you intend the premises to be used for the activity.
7. If the club wishes members and their guests to be able to consume alcohol on the premises please tick on, if the club wishes people to be able to purchase alcohol to consume away from the premises please tick off. If the club wishes people to be able to do both please tick both.
8. Please give information about anything intended to occur at the premises or ancillary to the use of the premises which may give rise to concern in respect of children, regardless of whether you intend children to have access to the premises, for example (but not exclusively) nudity or semi-nudity, films for restricted age groups etc gambling machines etc
9. Please list here steps you will take to promote all four licensing objectives together.
10. The application form must be signed.
11. This is the address which we will use to correspond with the club about this application.

Part A Club Premises Certificate
[Insert licensing authority details]

Club premises certificate number_____

Club details

Name of club in whose name this certificate is granted and relevant postal address of club_____

Post town_____Post code_____

Telephone number_____

If different from above the postal address of club premises to which this certificate relates, if any, or if none, ordnance survey map reference or description_____

Post town_____Post code_____

Telephone number_____

Where the club premises certificate is time limited the dates_____

Qualifying club activities authorised by the certificate_____

The times the certificate authorises the carrying out of qualifying club activities_____

The opening hours of the club_____

Where the certificate authorises supplies of alcohol whether these are on and/ or off supplies_____

Annex 1 - Mandatory conditions
Annex 2 - Conditions consistent with the Club operating Schedule
Annex 3 - Conditions attached after a hearing by the licensing authority
Annex 4 - Plans

Part B
Club Premises Certificate Summary
[Insert Licensing authority details]

Club premises certificate number_____

Club details

Name of club in whose name this certificate is granted and relevant postal address of club_____

Post town_____Post code_____

Telephone number_____

If different from above the postal address of club premises to which the certificate relates, or if none, ordnance survey map reference or description_____

Post town_____Post code_____

Telephone number_____

Where the club premises certificate is time limited the dates_____

Qualifying club activities authorised by the certificate_____

The times the certificate authorises the carrying out of qualifying club activities_____

The opening hours of the club_____

Where the certificate authorises supplies of alcohol whether these are on and/ or off supplies_____

State whether access to the club premises by children is restricted or prohibited_____

[Insert name and address of relevant licensing authority and its reference number (optional)]

Application to Vary a Club Premises Certificate Granted under the Licensing Act 2003

*[The form, as it appears in the Regulations is headed "Application to vary a club premises certificate **to be** granted under the Licensing Act 2003". The words "to be" appear to have been included in error.]*

PLEASE READ THE FOLLOWING INSTRUCTIONS BEFORE COMPLETING APPLICATION

Before completing this form please read the guidance notes at the end of the form. If you are completing this form by hand please write legibly in block capitals. In all cases ensure that your answers are inside the boxes and written in black ink. Use additional sheets if necessary.

You may wish to keep a copy of the completed form for your records.

(Insert name of club) club applies for [the variation of] a club premises certificate under section 84 of the Licensing Act 2003 for the premises named in Part 1 below

[The form, as it appears in the Regulations, omits the words "the variation of"; this appears to be an error.]

Club premises certificate number_____

Part 1 – Club premises details

Name of club_____

Postal address of premises, if any, or if none ordnance survey map reference or description_____

Post town _____Post code_____

Telephone number (if any)_____

E-mail address (optional)_____

Name of person performing duties of a secretary to the club_____

Address of person performing duties of a secretary to the club_____

Post town _____Post code_____

Daytime contact telephone number (if any)_____

E-mail address (optional)_____

Current postal address if different from premises address_____

Post town _____Post code_____

Part 2 – Applicant details

Daytime contact telephone number (if any)_____

E-mail address (optional)_____

Current postal address if different from premises address_____

Post town _____Post code_____

Part 3– Variation

Do you want the proposed variation to have effect   Please tick √ Yes
as soon as possible?   ☐

If not, do you want the variation to take effect from [Day Month Year]

If the club's proposed variation would mean that 5,000 or more people are expected to attend the premises at any one time, please state the number expected to attend_____

Please describe briefly the nature of the proposed variation (Please see guidance note 1)_____

Part 4 – Club Operating Schedule
Please complete those parts of the Club Operating Schedule which would be subject to change if this application to vary is successful.

What qualifying club activities do you intend to conduct on the club premises which will be affected by your application?

Provision of entertainment	Please tick √ Yes
a) plays (if ticking yes, fill in box A)	☐
b) films (if ticking yes, fill in box B)	☐
c) indoor sporting events (if ticking yes, fill in box C)	☐
d) boxing or wrestling entertainment (if ticking yes, fill in box D)	☐
e) live music (if ticking yes, fill in box E)	☐
f) recorded music (if ticking yes, fill in box F)	☐
g) performances of dance (if ticking yes, fill in box G)	☐
h) anything of a similar description to that falling within (e), (f) or (g) (if ticking yes, fill in box H)	☐

Provision of entertainment facilities for:
i) making music (if ticking yes, fill in box I)	☐
j) dancing (if ticking yes, fill in box J)	☐
k) entertainment of a similar description to that falling within (i) or (j) (if ticking yes, fill in box K)	☐

The supply of alcohol by or on behalf of a club to, or to the order of, a member of the club (if ticking yes, fill in box L) ☐

The sale by retail of alcohol by or on behalf of a club to a guest of a member of the club for consumption on the premises where the sale takes place (if ticking yes, fill in box L) ☐

In all cases complete boxes M, N, O and P

[Boxes A to M follow here; they are identical to those set out at pages 152–156 above and are not reproduced again here.]

O
Please identify those conditions currently imposed on the certificate which you believe could be removed as a consequence of the proposed variation you are seeking_____

_____

Please tick √ Yes
- I have enclosed the club premises certificate ☐
- I have enclosed the relevant part of the club premises certificate ☐

If you have not ticked one of these boxes please fill in reasons for not

including the certificate, or part of it below.
Reasons why the club has failed to enclose the club premises certificate or relevant part of it_____

P
Describe the steps you intend to take to promote the four licensing objectives:
a) General – all four licensing objectives (b,c,d,e) (please read guidance note 9)_____
b) The prevention of crime and disorder_____
c) Public safety_____
d) The prevention of public nuisance_____
e) The protection of children from harm_____

IT IS AN OFFENCE, LIABLE ON CONVICTION TO A FINE OF UP TO LEVEL 5 ON THE STANDARD SCALE UNDER SECTION 158 OF THE LICENSING ACT 2003 TO MAKE A FALSE STATEMENT IN OR IN CONNECTION WITH THIS APPLICATION.

Part 5 – Signatures (please read guidance note 10)
I [Insert full name] make this application on behalf of the club and have authority to bind the club.
Signature_____

Date_____ Capacity_____
Address for correspondence associated with this application (please read guidance note 11) _____

Post town_____Post code_____
Telephone number (if any)_____
If you would prefer us to correspond with you by e-mail your e-mail address (optional)_____

Notes for Guidance
1. Describe the premises. For example the type of premises it is, its general situation and layout and any other information which could be relevant to the licensing objectives. Where your application includes off-supplies of alcohol and you intend to provide a place for people to consume these off-supplies please include a description of where this will be and its proximity to the premises.
2. Where taking place in a building or other structure please tick as appropriate. Indoors may include a tent.
3. Please state type of activity to be authorised, if not already stated, and give relevant further details, for example (but not exclusively) whether or not music will be amplified or unamplified.
4. For example (but not exclusively) where the activity will go on for an extra hour during the summer months.
5. For example (but not exclusively), where you wish the activity to go on longer on a particular day, e.g. Christmas Eve.
6. Please give timings in 24 hour clock. (eg 16:00).
7. If the club wishes members and their guests to be able to consume alcohol on the premises please tick on, if the club wishes people to be able to purchase alcohol to consume away from the premises please tick off. If the club wishes

people to be able to do both please tick both.

8. Please give information about anything to occur at the premises or ancillary to the use of the premises which may give rise to concern in respect of children, for example (but not exclusively) nudity or semi-nudity, films for restricted age groups etc gambling machines etc

9. Please list here steps you will take to promote all four licensing objectives together.

10. The application form must be signed by someone with authority to bind the club.

11. This is the address which we will use to correspond with the club about this application.

[Insert name and address of relevant licensing authority and its reference number (optional)]

Application for the Review of a Premises Licence or Club Premises Certificate under the Licensing Act 2003

PLEASE READ THE FOLLOWING INSTRUCTIONS FIRST

Before completing this form please read the guidance notes at the end of the form. If you are completing this form by hand please write legibly in block capitals. In all cases ensure that your answers are inside the boxes and written in black ink. Use additional sheets if necessary.

You may wish to keep a copy of the completed form for your records.

I (insert name of applicant) [apply for the review of a premises licence under section 51] [apply for the review of a club premises certificate under section 87] of the Licensing Act 2003 for the premises described in part 1 below (delete as applicable)

Part 1 – Premises or Club premises details

Postal address of premises or club premises, or if none, ordnance survey map reference or description_____

Post town _____Post code (if known)_____

Name of premises licence holder or club holding club premises certificate (if known)_____

Number of premises licence or club premises certificate (if known)_____

Part 2– Applicant details   Please tick √ Yes

I am

1) an interested party (please complete (A) or (B) below)   ☐
   a) a person living in the vicinity of the premises   ☐
   b) a body representing persons living in the vicinity of the premises   ☐
   c) a person involved in business in the vicinity of the premises   ☐
   d) a body representing persons involved in business in the vicinity of the premises   ☐
2) a responsible authority (please complete (C) below)   ☐
3) a member of the club to which this application relates (please complete (A) below)   ☐

(A) DETAILS OF INDIVIDUAL APPLICANT (fill in as applicable)

Mr ☐   Mrs ☐   Miss ☐   Ms ☐   Other title (for example, Rev) ___

Surname _____First names_____

Please tick √ Yes

I am 18 years old or over   ☐

Current address_____

Post town _____Post code_____

Daytime contact telephone number_____

E-mail address (optional)_____

(B) DETAILS OF OTHER APPLICANT

Name and address_____

Telephone number (if any)_____

E-mail (optional)_____

(C) DETAILS OF RESPONSIBLE AUTHORITY APPLICANT

Name and address_____

Telephone number (if any)_____

E-mail (optional)_____

This application to review relates to the following licensing objectives

Please tick one or more boxes√

1) The prevention of crime and disorder ☐
2) Public safety ☐
3) The prevention of public nuisance ☐
4) The protection of children from harm ☐

Please state the ground(s) for review (please read guidance note 1)____

_____

Please provide as much information as possible to support the application
(please read guidance note 2)_____

_____

Please tick √ yes

Have you made an application for review relating to this
premises before? ☐

If yes, state the date of that application [Day Month Year]

If you have made representations before relating to this premises please
state what they were and when you made them_____

_____

Please tick √ Yes

- I have sent copies of this form and enclosures to the
  responsible authorities and the premises licence holder or
  club holding the club premises certificate, as appropriate ☐
- I understand that if I do not comply with the above
  requirements my application will be rejected ☐

IT IS AN OFFENCE, LIABLE ON CONVICTION TO A FINE OF UP TO LEVEL 5 ON THE STANDARD SCALE UNDER SECTION 158 OF THE LICENSING ACT 2003 TO MAKE A FALSE STATEMENT IN OR IN CONNECTION WITH THIS APPLICATION.

Part 3 – Signatures (please read guidance note 3)

Signature of applicant or applicant's solicitor or other duly authorised agent
(please read guidance note 4). If signing on behalf of the applicant,
please state in what capacity_____

Date_____ Capacity_____

Contact name (where not previously given) and address for

correspondence associated with this application (please read guidance note 5) _____

Post town_____Post code_____

Telephone number (if any)_____

If you would prefer us to correspond with you using an e-mail address your e-mail address (optional)_____

Notes for Guidance
1. The ground(s) for review must be based on one of the licensing objectives.
2. Please list any additional information or details for example dates of problems which are included in the grounds for review if available.
3. The application form must be signed.
4. An applicant's agent (for example solicitor) may sign the form on their behalf provided that they have actual authority to do so.
5. This is the address which we shall use to correspond with you about this application.

Form of Notice of Application for Registration under Part II,
Gaming Act 1968: Members' Club

To the Chief Executive of the Gaming Licensing Committee for the Petty Session of _____

I,_____, of _____ **HEREBY APPLY** for the registration under Part II of the Gaming Act 1968 of the club named _____ in respect of premises consisting of _____ (*give a sufficient description to identify the premises precisely*) situated at the following address: _____

The club is a *bona fide* members' club and is not carried on for any purpose other than those mentioned below. In particular it is not carried on for the private advantage of anyone other than the members generally. It has not less than twenty-five members and is not of a merely temporary character.

The purposes of the club are _____

[The club has not previously been registered under Part II of the Act in respect of these or any other premises.] [The Club has been registered under Part II of the Act previously.] [No previous registration has been cancelled (other than by relinquishment) and renewal of registration has never been refused.]

I am the _____ of the club and authorised to make this application on its behalf.

I understand that while the registration continues in force the officers of the club will be responsible for ensuring that no one takes part in gaming of any kind (apart from slot machines) on the premises at any time who is not genuinely a member of the club or a guest of a member (Gaming Act 1968 sections 12 & 23).

Dated the _____ day of _____ 20 __

Signed _____ [Applicant] [Authorised agent]

Note: Not later than seven days after the application is submitted, copies must be sent to the chief officer of police and the Collector of Customs and Excise.

Appendix B

Fees

The following fees are prescribed by the Licensing Act 2003 (Fees) Regulations 2005 (SI 2005 No. 79), the Licensing Act 2003 (Transitional Conversions Fees) Order 2005 (SI 2005 No. 80) and the Licensing Act 2003 (Fees) (Amendment) Regulations 2005 (SI 2005 No. 357).

- Conversion application during the transitional period – scale fee*
- Application for the grant of a club premises certificate – scale fee*
- Application for variation of a club premises certificate – scale fee*
- Request for a copy of certificate or summary....................£10.50
- Notification of change of name, address, or rules..............£10.50
- Each temporary event notice...£21.00
- Application for copy of temporary event notice................£10.50

* Scale fees are charged according to the non-domestic rateable value of premises as follows:

     Band A (rateable value £0 - £4,300)..................................... £100
     Band B (rateable value £4,301 - £33,000)............................£190
     Band C (rateable value £33,001 - £87,000)..........................£315
     Band D (rateable value £87,001 - £125,000)...................... £450
     Band E (rateable value £125,001 or over)............................£635

Premises that do not have non-domestic rateable values are treated as included in Band A.

Additional fees are payable by clubs that have 5,000 or more persons present on club premises when licensable activities take place. Fees are also increased for clubs which are "relevant premises", i.e., premises used exclusively or primarily for the supply of alcohol for consumption on the premises.

Annual fee

     Band A (rateable value £0 - £4,300)..................................... £70
     Band B (rateable value £4,301 - £33,000)............................£180
     Band C (rateable value £33,001 - £87,000)..........................£295
     Band D (rateable value £87,001 - £125,000)...................... £320
     Band E (rateable value £125,001 or over)............................£350

Appendix C

Template for Club Rules

The aims and objectives of members' clubs are diverse. It is not possible to produce a set of rules that can be adopted by all clubs. This template gives an indication of the basic rules that ought to feature in the rules of a well run members' club. Particular attention has been paid to rules that must be included if the club is to satisfy the qualification criteria set out in the Licensing Act 2003; they are in italic type. Individual clubs will need to consider the way in which they are managed and add any additional provisions that are necessary to avoid any misunderstandings or uncertainties.

RULES OF THE [*insert the name or title of the club*]
[insert date on which the rules became effective]

1. Name, Address, Status and Objectives
Set out the name of the club and the address of the club's premises.

If the club is affiliated to a parent association or registered as a provident or friendly society, or if it is a miners' welfare institute, set out the details of the registration etc., and state whether the club is required to observe any national rules or regulations as a consequence.

Set out the aims and objects of the club, e.g., the promotion of sporting fellowship, or to provide the facility for social intercourse between members.

2. Use of Club Name
Specify the club name and how it is to be used in official publications of the club, on advertisements for the club and in relation to other club business, e.g., on letterheads, receipts and invoices.

3. The Management of the Club
This rule should set out the fact that the club is to be managed by a management committee responsible for its day to day running. It should

include such detail as the manner in which committee members are to be nominated and elected; whether elected officers are to be *ex officio* members of it; the duration of office of committee members; the responsibilities to be undertaken by the committee; the extent of its delegated powers; and whether retiring members are eligible for re-election.

The rule should also specify the frequency with which the committee is to meet; the procedures to be followed at committee meetings; how many members should be in attendance to establish a quorum; and the need to keep records that can be made available to the members. For example, the rule might specify that a third of the members should retire each year but be eligible for re-election; that in the event of a deadlock following any vote of the members, the chairman should have a deciding vote; and that minutes of the meeting are to be kept and published to the members.

Other management procedures may need to be dealt with, depending on the needs of the particular club.

4.   Finance

This rule should form the basis upon which the club's financial affairs are managed and accounted for. It should deal with the way in which banking facilities are to be set up and who should have the authority to conduct financial transactions on behalf of the club. For example, the rule might provide that the club's financial transactions should be the responsibility of the management committee but that cheques, receipts and other financial documents may be signed by the officers or any two of them.

The rules should also deal with such matters as the appointment and remuneration of auditors.

To comply with the qualifying conditions set out in the Act, the rule should require the keeping of proper, audited, books of account and specify the arrangements for informing the members about the finances of the club. Any provisions or arrangements under which property or monies of the club may be applied otherwise than for the benefit of the club as a whole, or for charitable, benevolent or political purposes, should also be set out in this rule.

5.   Officers

The rules should include specific details as to the officers the club should have; how each is to be elected or appointed; their terms of office; and the scope and extent of their duties. There may be different rules in respect of different officers. For example, a club may find it convenient to have separate rules relating to the chairman, the secretary and the treasurer.

Some clubs may need to have rules relating specifically to presidents of the club and club trustees.

6.   Membership

This rule is, perhaps, one of the most important since it is indicative of whether the club is established and conducted in good faith and, therefore, a qualifying club for the purposes of the Act. This rule should deal with the types of membership that are to be available. A separate rule or sub-rule might be drawn up for each category. For example, there may be separate provisions relating to full members, associate members, temporary members, family members and honorary members.

In each case the rules must make clear that no person may be admitted to membership, or allowed the privileges of membership, unless a period of not less than two days has elapsed between nomination or application and admission. This is a specific requirement of the Act.

These rules should make clear the rights of each class of member, especially in relation to attendance at general meetings and entitlement to vote.

Generally, all full members of a club should be entitled to attend general meetings and they should all have the right to vote. They should have equal voting rights and no one member should have a casting vote. All full members should be eligible for nomination for, and election to, office and to club committees.

7. General Meetings

The rules should make specific provisions in relation to general meetings of the members. The frequency of such meetings should be specified and the manner in which business should be conducted at them should be spelt out. For example, the rule should make clear that any suggestion that a change should be made to rules or to the way in which the club is managed must be put before the members in the form of a resolution, and that the resolution will be passed only if it has the support of the majority of members attending the meeting.

The rule should also allow for amendment to resolutions. It should provide for the quorum needed before any business can be transacted. It should make specific provisions for calling special or extraordinary meetings of the members. For example, it might provide for the officers of the club to call such meetings and for a special meeting to be called at the request of a given number of members (perhaps twenty members or ten per cent of the members).

8. Intoxicating Liquor

The rules of a club which includes the sale and supply of alcohol among its licensable activities should deal with how that activity is to be controlled.

Any arrangement that has the effect of restricting the club's freedom in relation to the purchase of alcohol may be taken into account by a licensing authority when deciding whether the club is established and conducted in good faith. Care should be taken to see that the rules do not impose such a restriction on the club.

The rules should specify the hours during which intoxicating liquor may be sold or supplied, and should specify the club's authority to supply guests of members, and whether the supply is to be for consumption on or off the premises.

The rules should also make clear that there are no arrangements for any person to receive any commission, percentage or similar payment on, or with reference to, the purchase of alcohol. This is an additional provision of the Act which is designed to ensure that the club is, in truth, a members' club and not one that is run for the benefit of a proprietor.

9. Guests

A club should have a rule that specifies whether members are to be allowed to introduce guests, and any restriction to be imposed on that right. For example, the rule might provide for the introduction of guests but state that no member may introduce more than two guests at any one time, and may not introduce the same guest more than six times in any period of twelve months. The object of such a limit is to ensure that a situation does not arise in which the number of guests present on club premises greatly exceeds the number of members present.

The rule should also make clear that while on club premises guests must behave in a proper fashion and comply with club rules. It should also make the member introducing the guest responsible for the guest's conduct while on the premises.

10. Functions for Non-members

A club may have premises which are an excellent venue for functions such as weddings, birthday celebrations or seminars. The members of the club may be content for the premises to be hired out for functions for non-members from time to time, to raise funds. Where this applies, the rules should state that the premises may be made available in such a way, and how often.

If such a power is used to too great an extent, a licensing committee may conclude that the club is not a genuine members' club and therefore ceases to be qualified for a club premises certificate.

11. Other Licensable Activities

The advent of the 2003 Act brings with it a situation in which licensable activities other than the sale and supply of alcohol are authorised by a club premises certificate. The rules of the club should now reflect the wishes of the members in respect of those activities. For example, they should state how and when entertainment is to be provided for members. The rules should also contain provisions in relation to any gaming which the club is authorised to allow under the Gaming Act 1968.

12. Discipline

From time to time a club may need to take disciplinary action against a member who is disruptive, who refuses to comply with club rules or otherwise acts in a way likely to bring the club into disrepute. The members should decide how they wish these matters to be dealt with and who should have power to take action. The wishes of the members in this respect should be set out clearly in the rules. For example, punishment for offending might include expulsion or temporary suspension.

A club may appoint a special group of members to act as a disciplinary committee or it may delegate disciplinary power to the chairman or some other officer. Some clubs might prefer for such matters to be dealt with by the members in general meeting, but such an arrangement might not be appropriate in urgent cases.

The diversity of club needs was referred to at the beginning of this appendix. This template is not intended to be a comprehensive guide to the rules a club should adopt. The members of each club must give thought to its aims and objectives and how they wish it to be run. There may be a variety of other issues that particular clubs need to include in their rules. They should be added, taking care that each rule is expressed in clear and unambiguous terms. For example, rules might be required in relation to the payment of subscriptions and the effects of non-payment; the extent to which young persons may be allowed to use club premises; and the eligibility of staff for membership of the club.

A club that is affiliated to a national organisation may be able to obtain a set of recommended rules from its head office. The Club and Institute Union may also be able to advise on rules that might be adopted by their member clubs.

Index